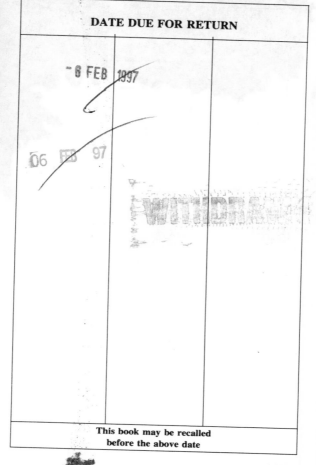

Threads
Cable-strong

Threads
Cable-strong

William Faulkner's *Go Down, Moses*

Dirk Kuyk, Jr.

Lewisburg
Bucknell University Press
London and Toronto. Associated University Presses

© 1983 by Associated University Presses, Inc.

345106

Associated University Presses, Inc.
4 Cornwall Drive
East Brunswick, N.J. 08816

Associated University Presses Ltd
27 Chancery Lane
London WC2A 1NF, England

Associated University Presses
Toronto M5E 1A7, Canada

Library of Congress Cataloging in Publication Data

Kuyk, Dirk, 1934–
   Threads cable-strong.

   Bibliography: p.
   Includes index.
   1. Faulkner, William, 1897–1962. Go Down,
Moses.   I. Title.
PS3511.A86G635   1982   813'.52   81-72030
ISBN 0-8387-5037-0

Printed in the United States of America

To Winkie

Contents

Acknowledgments

The following excerpts are reprinted by permission:
From *Go Down, Moses* by William Faulkner. Copyright 1940, 1941, 1942 by William Faulkner. Copyright 1942 by The Curtis Publishing Co. and renewed 1968, 1969, 1970 by Estelle Faulkner and Jill Faulkner Summers. Reprinted by permission of Random House, Inc.
"Go Down, Moses" in *The Book of American Negro Spirituals* by James Weldon Johnson and J. Rosamond Johnson. Copyright 1925 by The Viking Press, Inc., copyright renewed 1953 by Grace Nail Johnson, J. Rosamond Johnson and Lawrence Brown. Reprinted by permission of Viking Penguin, Inc.

My thanks especially to Paul Smith and James H. Wheatley for discussing *Go Down, Moses* and my manuscript with me. I also appreciate Florence Norkin's care in preparing the manuscript.

1 / "Was"

By tacking the phrase *and Other Stories* onto the title of William Faulkner's *Go Down, Moses,* some editor at Random House neatly indicated the apparent problem: is the book a novel or a collection of short stories? It looks like a collection. Its seven sections have titles as stories do. In fact, three sections and parts of two others had been published separately as stories before Faulkner revised them for incorporation into *Go Down, Moses.* He had unsuccessfully offered another for publication, and shortly after the book came out in 1942, magazines printed the remaining two sections as stories. Furthermore, *Go Down, Moses* lacks the kinds of unity readers expect in novels. It tells a variety of stories one after another rather than developing one in rich detail or even intertwining a number of them. It has a single setting, Yoknapatawpha County, but ranges across a period from 1807 to 1941. Far from treating events in chronological order, it jumps bewilderingly back and forth across the years. There are radical shifts of tone. The book focuses on no single character; and although six sections portray events in the lives of descendants of Lucius Quintus Carothers McCaslin, the main character in "Pantaloon in Black" is not a member of that family.

Faulkner himself called *Go Down, Moses* a novel. Insisting on having the addition deleted from the title when the book was reissued in 1949, he wrote his agent:

> I remember the shock (mild) I got when I saw the printed title page. . . . nobody but Random House seemed to labor under the impression that GO DOWN MOSES should be titled "and other stories" . . . Moses is indeed a novel. (Blotner, p. 1102)

Yet even his view of its genre was not always so clear-cut. In proposing the book to his publisher in 1940, Faulkner described it as "in method similar to *The Unvanquished*" (Blotner, p. 1043) and then as stories out of which "I can make a more or less continuous narrative" (Blotner, p. 1048). By 1941, when he was well into the creation of *Go Down, Moses,* he called it "collected short stories" (Blotner, p. 1072).

The question of what label to pin on the book is trivial, but the effort to answer the question springs from the reader's justifiable desire to understand the experience of reading *Go Down, Moses.* Having learned the only lesson that experience teaches—"Expect to meet what you have met before"—readers look for the firm ground of the familiar. They desire to find works of literature meaningful and whole, but where and how they will look for meaning and unity depend upon what they conceive to be the nature of the work. Those who expect *Go Down, Moses* to be a novel will search harder for whatever ties sections together than will those who expect only stories.

Readers, however, learn in literature, as the prudent do in life, that the lesson of experience has a corollary: expect the unexpected. While satisfying some expectations, *Go Down, Moses* may do what all good literature does. It may meet many expectations in unanticipated ways; it may leave other expectations unsatisfied, like false leads in a mystery; and it may meet requirements of its own that the reader never foresaw. *Go Down, Moses* takes us, I think, into the unfamiliar and therefore hazardous middle ground between novels and collections of stories. While we continue to look for meaning and unity, we are much less certain than usual about the forms they can take there. Yet readers who know Faulkner's earlier books should expect such uncertainty too, because since the late 1920s he had been experimenting with form, especially with forms that integrate fragments, sometimes successfully as in *The Sound and the Fury* and *As I Lay Dying,* sometimes not so successfully as in *The Wild Palms. Go Down, Moses* may be among the most daring of these experiments. Earlier works had achieved unity through conventional focusing—on the Compson family, on the Bundrens' journey to bury Addie, on the character and motives of Thomas Sutpen, and on the rise of Flem Snopes—and through juxtapositions—Joe Christmas against Lena Grove, the stories in *The Wild Palms* against one another. *Go Down, Moses,* however, refuses to allow us a clear focus or simple juxtapositions and yet compels us by a multitude of devices to try to unify the text, both while we read it and afterwards when we contemplate our experience of reading it.

How does *Go Down, Moses,* despite its obvious fragmentation, come to seem whole? Many readers must have sensed some kind of unity; otherwise, they wouldn't have sought its unifying principles. In puzzling over this problem, critics have naturally settled on the two common sources of unity: patterns of action and thematic parallels. Olga Vickery, for instance, called *Go Down, Moses* a "loosely constructed novel" in which "the framework of each . . . story is a ritual hunt" (124), and Cleanth Brooks saw the book as a history of the McCaslin family (244). Critics innumerable have pointed out themes that run through the book, particularly those about interracial relationships and about the destruction of the wilderness. Although these interpretations seldom seem wrong, they never seem adequate. Each of them sacrifices too much by abstracting simple patterns of action or theme from a complicated text. But how else can one talk about the book? Perhaps by not abstracting so much so soon, by beginning with and for a long time sticking close to the experience of reading the text. Let's see what happens if we look closely at the first four paragraphs of *Go Down, Moses.* The text begins:

WAS

Isaac McCaslin, 'Uncle Ike', past seventy and nearer eighty than he ever corroborated any more, a widower now and uncle to half a county and father to no one (3)

On beginning to read a work, nobody can tell what
deserves remembering. This passage, even though it begins without indentation and ends without a period,
forms the text's first unit. How do I go about reading it? I
come to the text with no clear-cut formula for understanding it but with a multitude of possibilities. Reading is
characterized by uncertainty, by trial and error, by the
gauging of probabilities—in short, by the ability to learn.
Although what I have learned from reading *Go Down,
Moses* over and over has by now erased my memory of
how strange and confusing the book must have seemed
when I first read it, I want to pretend to be a first-time
reader, no doubt one far more alert than I really was. Such
a pretense will show how quickly the narrative plunges its
reader into difficulties and how the reader strives to solve
them.

Isaac McCaslin

Is this the main character? Of "Was" or of the book?
Does his Christian name allude to the biblical Isaac? If so,
is the allusion straightforward? If it is ironic, how is it so?
(It will turn out that I should have emphasized the last
name, *McCaslin*.)

'Uncle Ike'

Who has the right or the temerity to call him "Uncle"
and "Ike"? Is the narrator a niece or a nephew, or does the
epithet express disrespect or maybe indicate that "Uncle
Ike" is as benevolent as a Dutch uncle?

past seventy and nearer eighty than he ever corroborated any
more

What is the significance of his age? Is it related to the
title "Was"? Why doesn't he corroborate his age?

a widower now and uncle to half a county and father to no
one

There is plainly an objective, third-person narrative
voice here, one that conveys facts ("Isaac McCaslin . . . a
widower now"). But the single quotation marks around
" 'Uncle Ike' " indicate the presence of another "voice,"
one that expresses society's attitudes (" 'Uncle Ike' . . .
uncle to half a county"). While the third-person voice runs
steadily along, reporting and authenticating everything in
the narration, the voice of society joins in here and there.
Rather than reporting words and acts, it pronounces the
judgments of society and conveys attitudes that may differ, as the single quotation marks show, from those of the
objective narrator. I wonder whether these two voices
speak the last words, "father to no one," in unison but
with different meanings, the objective voice indicating
simply that Ike has no child and the voice of society implying that Ike is somehow sterile.

Why the peculiarities of style? They clearly call attention
to themselves. Does the lack of indentation imply that the
narrative was going on before I tuned in? Does the failure
to complete a sentence keep the passage suspended, to be
resumed later?

The second paragraph begins without a capital letter:

this was not something participated in or even seen by himself

What does "this" refer to? Its lack of an antecedent suggests again the tuning in on a continuing narrative. I
gather that Ike will not be the main character of the coming story, unless in some deeper sense than actor or
witness.

but by his elder cousin, McCaslin Edmonds, grandson of
Isaac's father's sister and so descended by the distaff, yet
notwithstanding the inheritor, and in his time the bequestor,

of that which some had thought then and some still thought
should have been Isaac's, since his was the name in which the
title to the land had first been granted from the Indian patent
and which some of the descendants of his father's slaves still
bore in the land. (3)

This passage brings in more terms signifying family relationships. Here a third voice, that of the family, seems to
recite Cass's genealogy and the family's history. The use
of *McCaslin* as a first name indicates that the Edmondses
look up to the McCaslins. Society's voice gossips about
whether Ike or Cass should have inherited the family
land. The county's memory extends further back than
Ike's years. Implied in the gossip are some of society's
conventions governing the possession of property. One
can bequeath land to which one has title. Since in-
heritances normally pass through the males in a family,
Cass's descent "by the distaff" makes his inheriting the
land an anomaly. This expression of society's skepticism
about who has a right to the land stirs doubts about the
legitimacy of the family's original title "granted from the
Indian patent." The voice of society also touches on the
racial composition of the county: whites, Indians (at least
in the past), and the McCaslin slaves' descendants, whom
the voice does not call Negro or black. What is meant by
"his was the name . . . which some of the descendants of
his father's slaves still bore in the land"? The passage
seems to say that many descendants of the family's slaves
are now named McCaslin. Since slaves who had no surnames often took their masters' names when freed, that
interpretation looks reasonable. Nevertheless, it proves
wrong: all the descendants with surnames are named
Beauchamp. Here the voices of society and the family may
again speak in unison, saying that the descendants, no
matter what their surname, still bear "in the land" the
name of McCaslin because both society and the family
know them to be McCaslins, although in what sense they
are McCaslins remains unclear.

But Isaac was not one of these:—a widower these twenty years, who in all his life had owned but one object more than he could wear and carry in his pockets and his hands at one time, and this was the narrow iron cot and the stained lean mattress which he used camping in the woods for deer and bear or for fishing or simply because he loved the woods; who owned no property and never desired to since the earth was no man's but all men's, as light and air and weather were; who lived still in the cheap frame bungalow in Jefferson which his wife's father gave them on their marriage and which his wife had willed to him at her death and which he had pretended to accept, acquiesce to, to humor her, ease her going but which was not his, will or not, chancery dying wishes mortmain possession or whatever, himself merely holding it for his wife's sister and her children who had lived in it with him since his wife's death, holding himself welcome to live in one room of it as he had during his wife's time or she during her time or the sister-in-law and her children during the rest of his and after (3–4)

Contradicting previous talk of Ike's having been dispossessed, the voice of the character Ike says that he "owned no property and never desired to since the earth was no man's but all men's." His voice rejects "will . . . chancery dying wishes mortmain possession," society's litany of conventions for possession. According to the voice of fact, Ike has never taken possession of the bungalow that is doubly his, as a wedding present to his wife and himself and as her bequest. Ike, in his word, merely "holds" it for his wife's sister and her children. The word "holding" briefly shifts the narrative's temporal perspective from the past toward the future, the rest of his time and after.

not something he had participated in or even remembered except from the hearing, the listening, come to him through and from his cousin McCaslin born in 1850 and sixteen years his senior and hence, his own father being near seventy when Isaac, an only child, was born, rather his brother than cousin and rather his father than either, out of the old time, the old days (4)

Beginning with a repetition from the second paragraph, the narrative emends its meditative chant by replacing "seen" with "remembered," emphasizing that only through memory can we comprehend the past that still lives, the "was" that is. "Hearing" and "listening" show that McCaslin Edmonds has told the tale to Ike, whose memory is the source of the text. The family's recitation of relationships is expanded. The possible allusion to the biblical Isaac is strengthened because Ike was born in his father's old age, but then it is weakened because Ike was an only child. The relationships gain a metaphorical power in the sequence "rather his brother than cousin and rather his father than either." With a reference to the depths of time from which this memory comes, Part 1 breaks off without a period. Will this narration be resumed later?

The style of Part 1 is rhetorical: it is both showy and highly patterned. Its most striking traits are its loose grammatical form and, almost contradictorily, its frequent parallelism. On the one hand, it leaves sentences unfinished or lets them sprawl. It omits capital letters and suppresses punctuation. On the other, it balances groups of words, and the groups themselves often contain subordinate parallels. The vocabulary ranges from sonorous polysyllables like "bequestor" to colloquial phrases like "ease her going." The style frequently uses structures that offer terms, negate them, and substitute other terms as in "the earth was no man's but all men's" and "rather his brother than cousin and rather his father than either." As these last phrases show, the style is also rich in patterns of sound.

Against this rhetoric the style of Part 2 stands out:

> When he and Uncle Buck ran back to the house from discovering that Tomey's Turl had run again, they heard Uncle Buddy cursing and bellowing in the kitchen, then the fox and the dogs came out of the kitchen and crossed the hall into the dogs' room and they heard them run through the dogs' room

into his and Uncle Buck's room then they saw them cross the
hall again into Uncle Buddy's room and heard them run
through Uncle Buddy's room into the kitchen again and this
time it sounded like the whole kitchen chimney had come
down and Uncle Buddy bellowing like a steamboat blowing
and this time the fox and the dogs and five or six sticks of
firewood all came out of the kitchen together with Uncle
Buddy in the middle of them hitting at everything in sight
with another stick. It was a good race. (4–5)

Again, a cryptic opening *in medias res*. Who is "he"?
Who are Buck and Buddy? In what way are they uncles?
Who or what is Tomey's Turl—can such a name signify a
person? What does "run" mean? Why is the event characterized as "a good race"?

Here rhetoric has given way to oral storytelling. The
voice, which isn't Cass's since Cass wouldn't refer to himself as "he," nonetheless employs the paratactic structure
"and . . . and . . . and" that children often use for stories.
Part 2 begins with a fast-paced scene of slapstick and with
hyperbolic images. This voice's tone and syntax, unlike
that of Part 1, implies that "Was" will be a comic tale.

These first four paragraphs foreshadow the difficulty
that a reader must face in *Go Down, Moses*. The narration
has portrayed only one act, the "race," but has named
many—inheriting, bequeathing, granting, owning, camping, holding, listening, and so on. These names and other
words have begun to form clusters in the narrative, and
the clusters have begun to shape areas of meaning. "Uncle," "sister," "widower," "father," "grandson," and
"cousin" signify family relationships. "Past seventy," "elder," and "sixteen years his senior" refer to age. "Indians"
clusters with "slaves"; another cluster gathers together
words denoting sex: not only all the family relationships
except "cousin" but also "distaff." Still another joins "inheritor," "bequestor," "title," "owned," "property,"
"gave," "chancery," and "willed" in a cluster having to do
with possession. In *Go Down, Moses* these areas of meaning—family relationships, age, race, sex, and posses-

sion—are dynamic; they intertwine. But they are static too; they hold still long enough to be identified. Thus in reading, one draws together bits of the text into tentative clusters; and as one reads further, one adds new bits to those clusters, forms new ones, and gathers clusters into larger and larger clusters. *Go Down, Moses* seems to employ three kinds of clusters, which I will call patterns of narration, patterns of action, and patterns of meaning.

A pattern of narration is a "voice" characterized by its style, information, interests, assumptions, tones, and so on. Stories normally seem to consist of two kinds of voices: the characters' voices speaking in quotations and the narrators' voices speaking elsewhere. The narration of *Go Down, Moses* is not so simple as that. So far I have suggested the existence of five patterns of narration—the voices of the third-person narrator, society, the McCaslin family, and the characters Ike and Cass—and others will be noted later. These voices need not take turns speaking. Any voice may dominate from time to time; it need not silence all the others. They can whisper, echo, and speak in unison; they can employ puns and irony. The overall narrative voice of *Go Down, Moses* is thus not a single voice but a chorus. It is the orchestration of voices of different colors, voices high and low, solos and duets and trios contrasting with the sound of the full chorus. In this intricate narration the reader must hear all the notes, dynamics, melodies, harmonies, counterpoint, and dissonances.

In the chorus the objective voice has a large part. It determines that the narrative will be in the third person. It presents names and background, conveys quotations, and implicitly authenticates all such information. Other voices can silence, subordinate, or join it. A character's voice chimes in, for example, when the character's consciousness influences the patterns of narration. That might occur in free indirect discourse or in such nameless ways as in Part 1 when Ike's views briefly affect the narrative. The narrative of Part 2 is mainly a duet consisting of Cass's voice and the objective narrator's. The voice of society is the voice of law, custom, ritual, public opinion, prejudice, and history—in short, of cultural axioms, attitudes, and beliefs. As a culture speaks through that voice, so the McCaslin family expresses its attitudes through the voice of the McCaslins. Distinguishing among these voices (and using capital letters to indicate dominant voices), I hear the first passage of "Was" like this:

Voice	
Objective	Isaac McCASLIN, 'Uncle Ike,' past seventy and nearer
Society	'UNCLE IKE'
McCaslins	McCaslin
Ike	
Objective	eighty than he ever corroborated any more, a widower
Society	
McCaslins	
Ike	
Objective	now and uncle to half a county and father to no one
Society	and uncle to half a county and father to no one
McCaslins	and father to no one
Ike	and father to no one

In saying "McCaslin," the objective voice simply gives the name; the family's voice indicates that "he is one of us." By saying "Uncle Ike," the objective voice records the nickname while society expresses its attitude toward the man. From voice to voice the connotations of the last phrase differ. The first voice merely asserts the fact, the second implies sterility, the third mourns the end of the legitimate McCaslin line, and the fourth expresses Ike's regret at having lost, by trying to save him, the son he had hoped to have (351). We experience this book's, or any book's, pattern of narration directly as the text itself. In *Go Down, Moses* the pattern is one source of unity: we hear its diverse voices as a chorus.

As the chorus conveys the narrative, however, the reader abstracts both patterns of action and patterns of meaning from the text; and it is on these patterns that I will concentrate from now on. A pattern of action is a conception of an act, an idea about how to define its shape and its nature. By saying, "It was a good race," the narration of Part 2 of "Was" assigns a pattern to the action by naming it and by indicating that it has ended. In addition, the narrative treats the act comically and romantically as a "good race," not ironically as chaos, satirically as folly, or tragically as an unfortunate delay.

Patterns of action take four forms, the first of which is ritual, a term used here in a much broader sense than is normal. By *ritual* I mean much more than a religious rite. Here the word *ritual* refers to acts as a culture conventionally conceives of them. Racing, selling, hunting, and marrying would thus all be rituals because cultural conventions determine what one does to race, sell, hunt, or marry. How a character's acts are to be defined and understood depends on the culture in which they occur. Shared cultures mean shared rituals, shared conventions about the form and nature of acts. So far, so good. But in *Go Down, Moses* (and elsewhere) an act may come under the aegis of several sets of conventions—those of the character's culture, of his setting (since its conventions may differ for a character in an alien culture), of the writer's culture, and of the reader's. (Readers who cannot make these distinctions will naively impose their own conventions on all the world. The less American, rural, and Southern a reader's culture is, the more careful he may need to be while interpreting *Go Down, Moses*.)

Rituals, then, are another source of unity in *Go Down, Moses*. Among the kinds of rituals are the archetypal patterns of action as Northrop Frye has described them. These enable one to think of acts as quests that succeed or fail—that is, as romance or irony—or as the salvation of society through rejuvenation or through sacrifice—that is, as comedy or tragedy. There are rituals of opposition: the race, the hunt, the game of poker, the crap game, the duel, and even the lynching. There are rituals of the family: courting, marriage, building the fire on the hearth, seduction, birth, divorce, death, mourning, and burial. Rituals of the family also govern the behavior of bachelors and spinsters, of widows and widowers. There are ritual conceptions of the cycles of nature—"acorn oak and leaf and acorn again, dark and dawn and dark and dawn again in their immutable progression" (328–29)—and these conceptions serve as patterns of action: "Summer, then the bright days after the first frost, then the cold and himself on the wagon with McCaslin this time and the moment would come and he would draw the blood" (174–75). Another set of rituals is that of possession: bequeathing and inheriting, being dispossessed and expropriating, selling and buying, losing and winning, dowering and being dowered.

The plot as a pattern of action consists of acts arranged in the order in which they are narrated. Plot is the "story line"; it is not necessarily ordered causally or chronologically. Plot, which often unifies narratives, does not quite suffice to join Parts 2, 3, and 4 of "Was" with Part 1. Nor does it suffice to unify *Go Down, Moses*.

The third pattern of action, the fabula, does contribute to unifying not only "Was" but also the book. The *fabula*, as I will use the term, consists of the acts of the plot arranged in chronological order. Unlike rituals, which readers can find ready-made and accept as conventions, the fabula must be constructed by abstracting its elements from the text. As we read, we try to put events into chronological order. Thus, consciously or subconsciously, we devise the fabula. Devising it must be an almost essential interpretive act because the fabula reveals exactly "what happens when" in the plot and is therefore essential to understanding motives, causes, and consequences. Without seeing the fabula, the reader cannot appreciate framing, flashbacks, and all the other nonchronological arrangements within stories; and, of course, anyone who fails to see such designs will miss their thematic significance as well. The fabula of *Go Down, Moses* extends

from old Carothers McCaslin's birth in 1772, the earliest
date that I can fix in the McCaslin family's chronology, to
November 1941.

History, the fourth pattern of action, is the line of time
running back into the depths of the past and presumably
running on into the future. The narrative of *Go Down,
Moses* sets its rituals, plot, and fabula in history that
reaches back through the discovery of the New World and
the fall of Rome to the moment of the Creation in the mind
of God.

Go Down, Moses is hard to understand partly because of
the difficulty of constructing its fabula. This difficulty
dawns slowly during a first reading of the book. The sequence (1, 2, 3, 4, 5) of material in the fabula of "Was"
undergoes a considerable deformation in the narrative (2,
4, 3, 5, 1):

Fabula of "Was"

Date	Acts	Position in Narrative
1859	Fox and dogs. Chase of Turl. Supper at "War-wick." Cass talks with Turl. Buck sets dogs after Turl. Bet. Ambush at Tennie's. Turl escapes. Buck in Sophonsiba's bed.	2 pp. 4–21
1859	Buck's poker game.	4 pp. 21–25
1859	Cass goes to get Buddy and tells him about the game.	3 p. 21
1859 early	Buddy's game. Return home. Fox and dogs.	5 pp. 25–30
1940s	Introduction to "Was"	1 pp. 3–4

The deformation, however, isn't noticeable enough to
be distracting. Although the narrative skips Buck's poker
game, Cass promptly fills the gap by telling Buddy what
had happened. That Part 1 is out of place can easily be
overlooked since the rest of "Was" moves so swiftly and
ends with another foxhunt in the house, a scene that appears to round off "Was" although it actually frames only
Cass's story. The next section of *Go Down, Moses* does not

seem at first to require integration with "Was." "The Fire
and the Hearth" introduces an Edmonds who is not Cass
and a "he" who is a new character, Lucas, a Beauchamp
who is black. Gradually readers notice threads—names,
events, dates, relationships—running through the stories
and realize—too late, the readers may fear—that they
need to construct not only a fabula for each story but also a
fabula for the book. Such construction calls for seeing both
chronological and causal relationships. Not knowing the
chronology is likely to lead to a muddling of motives since
causes must precede effects; yet knowing the chronology
invites fallacies *post hoc, propter hoc* in determining causes
and motives. Nevertheless, to be aware of the fabula, no
matter how deeply buried and even at times impossible to
uncover, is to sense a unifying element in the book.

Patterns of meaning assume two forms: motifs and
themes. Motifs are conventional patterns of meaning that
take such forms as cultural axiom, authoritative dictum,
prejudice, common sense, or scientific truth. One set of
motifs depends on the concept of opposites: black/-
white/Indian, elder/younger, man/woman, master/
slave, and God/man. Another set of motifs reflects beliefs
about roles and relationships within families. Attitudes
toward nature also create motifs. Hunters, for instance,
share a vision of the wilderness and salute it around their
campfires, "drinking not of the blood they spilled but
some condensation of the wild immortal spirit" (192). The
cycles of nature give rise to such beliefs as expressed by
Molly Beauchamp's phrase "the ground crying to get
planted" (62) and Cass's assertion that "the earth dont
want to just keep things, hoard them; it wants to use them
again" (186). Attitudes toward possession conflict with
one another in *Go Down, Moses*, these attitudes being expressed in the motifs of creating, holding, owning, taming, sharing, and relinquishing.

A theme is devised, as the fabula is, by abstracting it
from the text. As the reader arranges the welter of action
into the fabula, so the theme is worked out from a tangle

of meanings. It is often difficult, though, to see how to
work out the theme—that is, to see what principles to
apply in order to devise a theme adequate to a book's
complexity. One cannot do justice to *Go Down, Moses* by
treating it like a collection; too many links run through the
sections for that. Yet it is too fragmented to look like history or biography, the simplest notions of unity normally
applied to novels. A work can of course reveal its unity
and significance in other ways. As Jonathan Culler has
said, a work might use homologies, the pairing or the
synthesis of opposites, a common denominator, a series
with a summarizing or a transcendent final term, or an
explicit thematic statement (172–73). Some of these obviously might make promising hypotheses about how *Go
Down, Moses* is unified. Yet the work itself gives us clues,
as works always do, about what approaches to take.

The clues, which occur fairly often, are embodied in
images. The first is the image of "juxtaposed and reliefed."
In "The Fire and the Hearth" Roth's flashlight illuminates
Lucas and George on the Indian mound, which is like "a
photographer's backdrop before which the two arrested
figures gaped at him" (86). In "The Bear" campfire talk
leads Ike to envision the wilderness with "the men . . . and
the dogs and the bear and deer juxtaposed and reliefed
against it" (191). Even Ash has been "marked by the wilderness from simple juxtaposition to it" (202). In the commissary Ike and Cass stand "juxtaposed and alien now to
each other against their ravaged patrimony" (297–98).
"Delta Autumn" shows Ike's view of himself and Cass and
then of himself and his wife "juxtaposed not against the
wilderness but against the tamed land" (351). To read *Go
Down, Moses* is to "juxtapose and relief." One must juxtapose character to character—Ike and Cass, Sam and Lucas,
Lion and the fyce, and Gavin Stevens and Miss Worsham.
One must juxtapose character against scene—the Bear
against the wilderness, Sam against his cage that "aint
McCaslins" (167), Cass against the farm, and Lucas

against his fields in the middle of the farm. Ritual plays off against ritual, belief against belief.

The second clue is the image of "condensing and densifying." When Lucas is leading his mule through the creek bottom and toward the Indian mound, he senses that

> visibility seemed to have increased, as if the rank sunless jungle of cypress and willow and brier, instead of increasing obscurity, had solidified it into the concrete components of trunk and branch, leaving the air, space, free of it and in comparison lighter, penetrable to vision. . . .(37)

As the "composite" of two races, Lucas is not their battleground but a vessel "in which the toxin and its anti stalemated one another, seetheless, unrumored in the outside air" (104). His face is the "composite" of the faces of Confederate soldiers (108). In "The Old People" a buck looks "as if all of light were condensed in him and he were the source of it" (163); Sam is the "battleground" for his own mixed heritage (168); and while Sam and Ike wait for the buck, "there was a condensing, a densifying, of what he had thought was the gray and unchanging light until he realised suddenly that it was his own breathing, his heart, his blood—something, all things . . . " (182). In "The Bear" the commissary ledgers, "multiplied and compounded," chronicle the South (293), and Cass gestures

> so that, as the stereopticon condenses into one instantaneous field the myriad minutia [sic] of its scope, so did that slight and rapid gesture establish in the small cramped and cluttered twilit room not only the ledgers but the whole plantation in its mazed and intricate entirety. . . . (298)

To read *Go Down, Moses* is to compound and "densify" its patterns of narration, action, and meaning, superimposing them until their myriad minutiae condense and their jungle solidifies, until they become a source of light and visibility increases.

Juxtaposition and condensing oppose each other. Juxtaposition moves toward duality; condensing, toward unity. Yet to juxtapose is, in a sense, to unify: juxtapositions are balanced. On the other hand, to condense disparate material inevitably emphasizes the ways in which the material resists any neat fitting together. Juxtaposition and condensing are each nearly paradoxical: the one that aims at duality attains the unity of balance, and the one that seeks unity reveals the duality of incongruence. A book whose two basic forms of thought stand opposed to one another is likely to seem paradoxical; it is certainly unlikely to achieve a clear-cut resolution. Yet as Faulkner's readers know, he was never afraid of paradoxes or of endings that do not attain a neat synthesis. Indeed, paradox and a resistance to resolution seem to have been key qualities of his imagination, ones that determine in large measure the sort of books he wrote. In his imagination, however, I do not think that juxtaposition and condensing stood ultimately on equal footing. Faulkner normally emphasized condensation—that is, he chose not the balance of juxtaposition but the subtle incongruities that condensing reveals. His major novels superimpose viewpoint on viewpoint and play off style against style, plot against plot, and character against character but finally reject the simple balancing of juxtapositions and make the reader undertake the more demanding discriminations called for when viewpoints, styles, and so on are condensed. Using voices as patterns of narration, using ritual, plot, fabula, and history as patterns of action, and using motif and theme as patterns of meaning will enable us to begin to account for how juxtaposition and condensation stimulate the reader's sense of the unity of *Go Down, Moses*.

The style of Part 1 of "Was" makes the rest of the story's narration with its fast pace and superficially comic tone seem simple. The narration is dominated by a new voice, that of Cass as a boy. Its patterns of narration manifest themselves in ways other than parataxis. Hyperbolic images continue throughout the story—the horse with Buck astride it looking like "a big black hawk with a sparrow riding it" (8) and Buck holding the ribbon from Miss Sophonsiba "like it was a little water moccasin" (15). The wording is colloquial—"fetch," "free gift," "scrabbled," "cooter," and "back gallery"—and ponderosities of vocabulary are notably absent. Much dialogue, made memorable by its force and its epigrams, is narrated indirectly, as in "ladies were so damn seldom thank God that a man could ride for days in a straight line without having to dodge a single one" (7) and "any man who ever played poker once with Uncle Buddy would never mistake him again for Uncle Buck or anybody else" (7).

Although the voice of the character Cass has risen above the chorus, the other voices have not fallen silent. The objective voice, of course, continues reporting and authenticating. The voice of society often speaks in unison with Cass because he conceives acts in terms of society's rituals. Just as he thought of the ruckus in the house as "a good race," he conceives of the pursuit of Turl as a hunt and hopes to be in time to see him "treed" (8). Buck and Hubert Beauchamp share both the ritualizing view of the hunt and the vocabulary: they set dogs on Turl, "flush" him, see him "break cover," and, once they have lost his trail, plan to "bait for him" before he can "den." Turl's taking Buck to the Beauchamps' farm, however, makes the hunter into the hunted since Turl knows, as we and Buck and Buddy do, that Miss Sophonsiba and Hubert are laying traps for Buck. Turl sees himself as allied to women engaged in another ritual of opposition, the struggle between women and men. He says:

> I got protection now. All I needs to do is to keep Old Buck from ketching me unto I gets the word. . . . anytime you wants to git something done, from hoeing out a crop to getting married, just get the womenfolks to working at it. Then all you needs to do is set down and wait. (13)

His scheme begins to work when the trap slams shut on

Buck, who accidentally climbs into Miss Sophonsiba's bed in the dark. In telling Buck that he must marry her, Hubert talks the language of hunting:

> You come into bear-country of your own free will and accord. . . . you knew the way back out like you knew the way in and you had your chance to take it. But no. You had to crawl into the den and lay down by the bear. . . . You run a hard race and you run a good one, but you skun the hen-house one time too many. (22–23)

Buck counters by calling on another ritual of opposition, gambling. Hubert had bet $500 that Buck would catch Turl in Tennie's cabin, but Turl had escaped. Buck holds Hubert to the wager, and Hubert proposes a game of poker, the player with the lowest—that is, the losing—hand "winning" Sophonsiba and having to buy Turl or Tennie. When Buck loses, he sends Cass racing home for help and takes cover in the woods like a hunted animal. Buddy returns to stake Sophonsiba's dowry against Buck's freedom and wins through skillful wagering only after Hubert discovers that the supposedly disinterested dealer is Turl. Buck can remain a bachelor, the McCaslins buy Tennie, and she and Turl can marry. The story Cass tells ends with another foxhunt in the McCaslins' house, "a fine race while it lasted, but the tree was too quick" (30). Thus in "Was" the rituals of opposition, hunting and gambling, become involved with rituals of the family and of possession.

The chorus of voices that narrate "Was" poses questions and problems that challenge our power to answer them. These puzzles entice readers along and guide their efforts to interpret acts and meanings. Some take uncomplicated forms, an adverb pointing to an undefined "there" or a pronoun without an antecedent. Some puzzles are solved almost as quickly as they are posed:

> But Isaac . . . in all his life had owned but one object more than he could wear and carry in his pockets and his hands at

one time, and this was the narrow iron cot and the stained lean mattress. . . . (3)

Other puzzles, even ones posed at the beginning of "Was," take longer to solve. If Buck must hurry to catch Turl, why bother to get a necktie? Why had Buck and Buddy moved all the blacks into the big house? Only after finishing "Was" do we know the story to which the word *this* at the start of the second paragraph refers. Another puzzle involves three phrases that seem insignificant at first. A duet of voices, the narrator's and Cass's, indirectly quote Hubert's calling Turl "that damn white half-McCaslin" (6). The same pair of voices describes Turl's hands as "saddle-colored" (27); and when Hubert tilts the lampshade to see the dealer, the two voices again indirectly convey Hubert's perception as he recognizes "Tomey's Turl's arms that were supposed to be black but were not quite white" (29). (In "supposed" the voice of society indicates its standard, and the voice of the McCaslin family admits to having failed to meet the standard.) The enigma that the phrases point to is also highlighted by an act that might well puzzle a reader: since whoever gets the low hand will possess both Tennie and Turl, their marriage will apparently come about no matter who wins. Why then would Turl bother to stack the deck, as Hubert obviously believes he has done? This question is easy to answer once the reader realizes that Turl is actually the McCaslins' half-brother. He would simply rather be their slave than Hubert's.

Through the narrative voices, the rituals and beliefs serve to unify the story as the puzzles do. The voice of society emphasizes the archetypes of romance in the concept of conflict and in the ritual of the successful hunt. Society sees the story as one about ultimate victories in a series of rituals of opposition and possession. Cass enjoys an exciting hunt, and the white masters Buck and Buddy capture their runaway slave. Buddy's skill in poker wins Buck's freedom and a slave woman. From society's point of view the fact that Buddy's victory gains Turl the wife he sought is an extra comic frill.

If one hears no voice beyond the voices of society, Cass, and the third-person narrator, "Was" appears to be nothing more than a stereotypical antebellum tale stained by racism. The voice of the McCaslin family, however, assumes quite another tone. Cass's puzzlement over Turl's behavior begins to bring to the surface the conflict between society's attitudes and the family's. Cass says:

> Being a nigger, Tomey's Turl should have jumped down and run for it afoot. . . . But he didn't; maybe Tomey's Turl had been running off from Uncle Buck for so long that he had even got used to running away like a white man would do it. (9)

Society knows that Turl is a "white"—that is, light-colored—"half-McCaslin," as Hubert says; but because it believes that part-black is all-black, it expects Turl to follow the pattern of action conventional for slaves. Cass has not quite realized that the rituals and beliefs of the three McCaslin men partly violate those of society. Cass is, after all, only a boy and only an Edmonds. He sees but does not comprehend the rituals and beliefs peculiar to the family. Consequently Cass's voice, so strong in the narration, mutes but does not drown out the McCaslin voice.

The McCaslin voice reveals that the pursuit of Turl is a family ritual taking place about twice a year: Buck must wear a necktie, he knows where Turl is headed and why, and he fears that Turl, unless recaptured immediately, will be brought back by Hubert, accompanied by Sophonsiba. Society would have pursued Turl as an escaped criminal and would have dealt harshly with him if he frequently tried to escape. Buck and Turl act as if the pursuit is a hunt. Thus the family is unusual in fitting the pursuit into the ritual of hunting rather than into society's normal ritual. The Edmonds boy, himself a half-McCaslin, and even Hubert Beauchamp have come to share much of the family's view. The ritual allows Cass and Turl to talk during an interval in the hunt. The ritual permits setting dogs to track Turl but apparently precludes the use of guns and compels Buck to try to catch Turl with his bare hands. When Turl bursts from Tennie's cabin and runs over Buck, the quarry seems obliged to protect the hunter by easing his fall.

Buck and Buddy violate society's conventions in the way they treat all blacks, not just Turl. When they inherited the McCaslin farm from their father, they moved the slaves into his unfinished big house and built a cabin for themselves. Cass does not explain, perhaps does not know, what beliefs motivated this act. At this point the McCaslin voice volunteers no hints, and so the action, seen from a limited narrative viewpoint, is enigmatic.

Besides the voices of society, Cass, the third-person narrator, and the McCaslin family, there remains one voice. Inaudible on the first reading, the voice of Ike McCaslin becomes a continuing murmur on the second. What might the story Cass told at least forty years ago mean to Ike, who recalls it in his seventies? He knows that Buck's flight from Sophonsiba, which seems a triumph as Cass tells it, was a failure: about seven years later they were married. He may even regard the struggle to escape as wrongheaded; Buck and Sophonsiba are his parents. Ike has seen the dowry that Buddy staked against Buck's freedom pass to Buck, to himself, and then to Cass and Cass's descendants. With Ike the legitimate line of McCaslin men will die out; but Turl's marriage, peripheral in Cass's view, has resulted in children, grandchildren, and great-grandchildren, all named Beauchamp, but all "man-made" McCaslins. Ike knows that Buck and Buddy opposed slavery and had bought only one slave in their lives but had freed many. How then does he view their effort to ensure that Turl could be with Tennie by trying to sell him, their half-brother, to Hubert? How does Ike, who has come to regard hunting as "the best of all breathing" (192), react to considering the pursuit of Turl a hunt? Does Ike know at this point, as the second-time reader knows, that Cass's grandson and Turl's great-granddaughter have had an illegitimate son, their union paralleling the one between Ike's grandfather and Turl's grandmother and reuniting the two lines, the white and the "black," of the McCaslin family?

Like other puzzles in the book, some of these questions never yield to solution. Cass's romanticism is juxtaposed against Ike's irony, the cryptic silence of his voice. Does the title "Was" indicate his yearning for the good old days or his saying "good riddance" to the past? We never find out how he judged the tale or what patterns of action or meaning he ascribed to it. Even so, in his silence the mirth of Cass's narration dies away. It does so because, although Ike is silent, *Go Down, Moses* is not. Its choral narration and its patterns of action and meaning make Cass's story echo hollowly, and they darken its innocent—or mindless—optimism. The enigmas of narration, action, and meaning endure because of the text's ultimate penchant for condensing. It superimposes voices, acts, and meanings on one another until it overloads the reader's power to devise the equations, juxtapositions, and homologies that normally serve as unifying forms. Here, then, the final unifying act is superposition, the act of condensing and densifying.

2 / "The Fire and the Hearth"

The reader who expects *Go Down, Moses* to be a novel will find the transition from "Was" to "The Fire and the Hearth" a surprise. As the book combines these two independent stories, so "The Fire and the Hearth" contains revisions of two other stories previously published as "A Point of Law" and "Gold Is Not Always" and a third unpublished story called both "An Absolution" and "Apotheosis." These three stories, each with its own plot, form the three chapters of "The Fire and the Hearth" and make it resemble a collection. Because they do not continue the plot of "Was" but take up new characters in a new series of acts, they make the book seem a collection as well.

Yet the opening of "The Fire and the Hearth" obliges even readers who anticipate a separate story to look for links. In fact, the first sentence of "The Fire and the Hearth" implies a link and then deceptively withdraws the implication. The pronoun "he," lacking an antecedent, seems to refer to a character in "Was" but actually refers to Lucas Beauchamp. Still, the links exist. There are Edmondses again. Lucas deals with Roth, has struggled with Roth's father Zack, and remembers Cass. The indirect discourse that reveals Lucas's schemes reveals his feelings and his past, and suddenly his musings plunge us back into the McCaslin family's history. Memories of "Was" come pouring back. Lucas, we discover, lives on the Edmonds farm, the land Cass had somehow gotten from Ike. Lucas prides himself on being the oldest McCaslin descendant there. Time after time the plot is interrupted by the

history of the family from Carothers through Buck and
Buddy to Ike, through Cass and Zack to Roth, and
through "McCaslin slaves" to Lucas.

"The Fire and the Hearth" is a small-scale *Go Down,
Moses*. As the tangled narration makes the book a wilderness, "The Fire and the Hearth" is a thicket, smaller
but just as dense. Yet readers can penetrate it by using the
patterns that "Was" called for, the patterns of narration,
action, and meaning.

The choral narration invites us to push on. Again we
hear the voices of the third-person narrator and the
McCaslin family. Society's voice imposes social or cultural
patterns. In the courtroom it announces judicial deci-
sions—"Strike this off the docket" (129)—and enforces eti-
quette—"Take off your hat. . . . Say sir to the court" (128).
Public opinion adds to society's stock of fact when the
"minor annals of the town" record how Cass and Lucas,
"the white and the negro cousins" (109), go to the bank
side by side to deposit Lucas's legacy. Public opinion
stocks a supply of fantasy as well. The story of the $22,000
in the churn makes its rounds, and Lucas's carefully nur-
tured reputation as a near-teetotaler—"you or him or old
Cass either aint never heard of me having truck with any
kind of whisky except that bottle of town whisky you and
him give Molly Christmas" (60)—protects him in court
where the judge exclaims, "Lucas Beauchamp? . . . With
thirty gallons of whisky and a still sitting on his back porch
in broad daylight? Nonsense"(73).

But in the choral narration we hear new voices, too.
Lucas's voice makes itself audible above the third-person
narrator's in turns of phrase and in expressions of feelings
and memories, coloring the narrative in such places as I
have italicized:

> *It was not that he had anything against George personally*, despite
> the mental exasperation and the physical travail he was hav-
> ing to undergo *when he should have been at home in bed asleep. If*

> *George had just stuck to farming* the land which Edmonds had
> allotted him *he would just as soon Nat married George as anyone*
> *else, sooner than most of the nigger bucks he knew.*(34)

Lucas's simple vocabulary is juxtaposed to the third-
person narrator's rhetoric. Lucas's voice is most dominant
in "nigger bucks." There the established black McCaslin
expresses his contempt for the vulgar young George.

The voice of the Earth, another new sound in the
chorus, has only a small part in "The Fire and the Hearth."
Later in *Go Down, Moses* it will speak at greater length, but
never more directly. While Lucas is digging at the Indian
mound, he hears the Earth "whispering easily and steadily to the invisible shovel"; and when the "orifice" is deep,
the overhang collapses with what "was probably only a
sigh" but sounded as though the mound had "stooped
roaring down at him." Knocked over by the avalanche, he
listens to the subsequent "roaring wave of silence like a
burst of jeering and prolonged laughter"(38).

As the McCaslins' voice chimes in with Lucas's, so
along with the voices of Roth and Zack Edmonds we can
hear the antiphonal voice of the Edmonds branch of the
family. In Lucas's thoughts the McCaslins' voice sounds
strongly in the lists of family names, the consciousness of
the hereditary land, and the emphasis on society's belief
that the elder takes precedence over the younger and the
male over the female. The Edmondses share these beliefs
and consequently express subservience toward the branch
of the family that is older and descends through McCaslin
men, even when its racial heritage mingles black and
white. In pride of possession, self-assurance, and even
dress, Lucas probably bears the nearest likeness among
the McCaslins and the Edmondses to Carothers McCaslin.
Lucas views George as "an interloper without forbears"(40), scorns the sheriff as a "redneck without any
reason for pride in his forbears nor hope for it in his descendants" (43), and considers the Edmondses mere

"woman-made" members of the family. As their interior monologues show, the Edmondses accept his valuations, and he cows even Ike, who thinks:

> *Fifty dollars a month. He knows that's all. That I reneged, cried calf-rope, sold my birthright, betrayed my blood, for what he too calls not peace but obliteration, and a little food.*(108-9)

The book's narrative chorus is thus enlarged in "The Fire and the Hearth." The third-person narration speaks for itself and also reports the words of Lucas, Roth, Molly, Zack, Nat, George, and the minor characters. To the voices of society and the McCaslin family the story adds those of the Earth and the Edmondses.

On turning from patterns of expression to those of action, we find once again a greater complexity. Because each chapter has its own plot, the plot of "The Fire and the Hearth" as a whole is not immediately evident. Far from it. The first chapter tells how Lucas means to rid himself of George Wilkins, his daughter Nat's suitor and a bootlegger whose folly threatens Lucas's own moonshining business. Lucas aims to hide his still and then finger George. Through plan and counterplan the action moves fast, and by the chapter's end Lucas has been forced to let Nat and George marry and has accepted George as an apprentice moonshiner. In the second chapter Lucas gets a divining machine, a metal detector, by outsmarting a traveling salesman; and in the third Lucas's wife Molly forces him to relinquish the machine by threatening to divorce him. Each chapter can stand alone, as their separate publication indicates; yet eventually the reader discovers that each is a part of the whole story's larger plot concerning Lucas's fanatical search for buried treasure, his wife's even more fanatical opposition to that search, and his decision to give up the quest because he values his marriage beyond any treasure.

Within chapter 1 the moonshining plot actually obscures the larger plot. In trying to bury his still, Lucas chances upon a golden coin. He promptly shifts his aim; he will pursue the treasure. But his machinations have already stirred Nat and George to defend themselves by beating him to the punch. Overnight they put George's still and his jugs of whisky on Lucas's porch so that the next morning the sheriff and his men find both stills and arrest George, Nat, and Lucas. Only at the end of the chapter does Lucas succeed in securing their acquittals and thereby free himself to begin the treasure hunt.

Both plots in chapter 1 progress by means of rituals familiar from "Was"—that is, by patterns of action conventional within society or the family. Rituals of hunting and gambling crop up again. Here, as in "Was," the hunter falls into a trap. Lucas awakes in a bed too close to George's still; Buck got into bed with the "bear." Buck escaped through Buddy's skill in gambling and probably Turl's in cheating. Lucas—who is playing a more complex game against George, Nat, Roth, the sheriff, the court, and other prospective treasure hunters—has to rely on his own cleverness. Rituals of family life shape much of the action: Zack's wife dies, Roth is born, Molly nurses him along with her own son, Roth grows up and stays a bachelor, and George and Nat court and marry. Chapter 1 shares with "Was" the comic romance as an archetypal pattern of action. No matter what the deeper implications of "Was," on the surface it ends with the successful quest for a reintegrated society. In chapter 1 the quest also succeeds and unifies society. As Lucas's apprentice, George no longer threatens him; and despite some disagreement between George and Nat, the Beauchamps are no longer juxtaposed to one another but have condensed into a family that includes George. Yet this ending isn't final. It just leaves Lucas free to start another hunt, this time for treasure. Such a hunt is a ritual, too. Through memories of anthropologists digging into the Indian mound, through the tale of the $22,000 churn, and through a thousand Southern legends of treasure buried at the approach of Yankee troops, society has established the hunt's conventions—speed, secrecy, tattered maps, rotting containers, and bright cascades of silver.

Patterns of meaning intertwine with patterns of expression and action in the opening pages of "The Fire and the Hearth." Because voices are distinguished not only by how they speak but also by the attitudes they express, voices are partly defined by patterns of meaning, by motifs. In addition, the narrative keeps slipping away from the plots to express motifs of age, family, possession, sex, and race; and like "Was" it superimposes them on each other. One long paragraph, for example, advances the plot only minimally by saying that Lucas "knew exactly where he intended to go, even in the darkness." Then the paragraph introduces motifs of age and family: he knew the land because he had been born on it "twenty-five years before the Edmonds who now owned it" and because he had worked it all his life. Motifs of age, sex, and family appear when the narration says that Lucas had hunted rabbit and 'possum there too until he had decided that such hunting was "no longer commensurate with his status as not only the oldest man but the oldest living person on the Edmonds plantation." The next phrases present motifs of age, family, and race by calling Lucas "the oldest McCaslin descendant even though in the world's eye he descended not from McCaslins but from McCaslin slaves." Finally the paragraph uses motifs of age, family, and possession in saying that Lucas was "almost as old as old Isaac McCaslin who lived in town, supported by what Roth Edmonds chose to give him, who would own the land and all on it if his just rights were only known, if people just knew how old Cass Edmonds, this one's grandfather, had beat him out of his patrimony" (36).

Constantly alluding to the McCaslin family's history, the motifs connect patterns of meaning with patterns of action. One cannot grasp the meaning of an allusion without knowing the McCaslins' history. The reader must also contend with passages that are cryptic or even deceptive.

The third-person narrator's description of Lucas's land sounds paradoxical: " . . . it was his own field, though he neither owned it nor wanted to nor even needed to" (35). How can he not own "his own" field? Since his land is on the Edmonds plantation, how can he treat Roth so high-handedly? Why does Lucas consider himself a "McCaslin descendant even though in the world's eye he descended . . . from McCaslin slaves"? The narrative even raises once more the question from "Was": how did Cass get the McCaslin farm from Ike?

In moving on to the second part of chapter 1, the first-time reader has plenty to cope with—voices, acts (plots, rituals, and bits of history), and motifs (age, family, possession, sex, and race) as well as those enigmatic statements—and all these patterns connected to and superimposed on one another in ways that seem too complicated to be charted. The second part adds to the intricacy of the narrative by introducing new complexities. These would require me to stretch past any hope of belief the pretense, already violated, of being a first-time reader. Yet I think that my role, here cast aside, has served its end if it has suggested how readers begin to interpret so strange a text as *Go Down, Moses*. Finding that no familiar generic pattern organizes the narrative, readers pick out whatever threads they notice, and with the strongest threads they weave strands of voice, plot, ritual, fabula, history, motif, and theme. These strands they weave into the patterns of narration, action, and meaning that are cable-strong to bind the narrative together.

Now, in my true character as re-reader, I am able to look forward as well as back. It is necessary to glance both ways to see the significance of the second part of chapter 1. The part begins like a continuation of the first, with Lucas at Roth's to report the still; but as Roth steps out onto the gallery, Lucas's thoughts flash back forty-three years to Roth's birth and, more important, to Lucas's confrontation with Zack. Recounting the story of the birth in a single paragraph, the narrative tells how Zack's wife bore Roth on a night when a flood had torn away all the bridges and no doctor could be summoned. With Molly as midwife Roth was born, but the mother's condition grew critical. Risking his life to save her, Lucas swam the river before dawn and returned with a doctor by nightfall. But it was too late; the mother had died. Molly, who was nursing her son Henry, moved into Zack's house to nurse Roth too. She stayed there almost six months until Lucas demanded her back: "I wants my wife. I needs her at home. . . . I reckon you thought I wouldn't take her back, didn't you?" (46–47). That last sentence begins the account of the confrontation. The narrative lavishes space on that account—all of Part 2, nearly thirteen pages—and attention. Nowhere does "The Fire and the Hearth" more carefully analyze acts and motives. Yet since the account is not a part of any of the plots of "The Fire and the Hearth," what is its role? The confrontation, almost irrelevant to the story, has the deepest thematic significance for *Go Down, Moses*. It is an extraordinary intertwining of patterns of narration, action, and meaning; and only the re-reader can fully perceive its labyrinth of rituals, history, and motifs. Culture and family have jointly constructed a maze of oppositions that limit each character's range of action and vision. Their culture gives preference to men before women and to whites before blacks. Society, like Lucas, places "man-made" McCaslins before the "woman-made" Edmondses. Zack hesitates about passing his oath to "a nigger," and Lucas, thinking of killing Zack, considers how society will view the act.

> *He keeps her in the house with him six months and I dont do nothing: he sends her back to me and I kills him. It would be like I had done said aloud to the whole world that he never sent her back because I told him to but he give her back to me because he was tired of her. (49)*

Family ties bind Lucas firmly. They connect him inescapably with the Edmondses even to the point of his risking his life by swimming a flooded river to bring Zack's wife a doctor. He entered the river, as the narrative indirectly puts it, "not for his own sake but for that of old Carothers McCaslin who had sired him and Zack Edmonds both" (46). Hence behind Lucas and even behind Zack towers Carothers, who set the patterns that his descendants follow. Maintaining the fire on the hearth symbolizes for Lucas and for the narrative itself the stability of the family. The hearth is warmed by "a condensation not of fire but of time" (51). As Lucas looks back, he sees that mankind has regressed: in the old days there were "better men than these; Lucas himself made one" (44). When Zack keeps Molly in his house, Lucas sees him, although the first-time reader cannot, as Carothers reincarnated with Eunice or Tomasina at his side. Carothers looms so large that he may block Lucas's sight. Zack is not following Carothers's pattern, the ritual of sexual relations between the white man and the black woman. When Lucas says, "I reckon you thought I wouldn't take her back," implying that Molly had been Zack's mistress, the notion astonishes Zack. "So that's what you think," he says. "What kind of a man do you think I am?" (47). Lucas's answer may be inferred: a man like Carothers. Edmonds, however, offers his word of honor that Molly was not his mistress, and I judge that true. Realizing that his suspicions might be wrong, Lucas is not relieved but coldly contemptuous: *And that's a man!* (49). Zack would have earned his respect as well as his hatred by following Carothers's pattern. When Molly comes home with their son and Zack's, Lucas hopes to get satisfaction by making Zack ask for his son as Lucas went to demand his wife. But when Zack doesn't come, probably because in his eyes Molly is simply a wet-nurse, Lucas, always the McCaslin, still wants vengeance. He takes his straight razor and slips into the bedroom where Zack is sleeping. Lucas, however, has not yet worked himself up to murder. Against the tide of his enmity runs a deeper, warmer current: his lifelong friendship with Zack, "the man whom he had known from infancy, with whom he had lived until they were both grown almost as

brothers lived" (55). In this friendship Zack violates society's belief: to the sheriff, for instance, "Lucas was just
another nigger" (43). But Zack is faithful to his family's
attitudes and does not obey the racial conventions of his
culture. Lucas's and Zack's lives as well as their family's
history link them. Lucas rejects one ritual of opposition:
although he carries his straight razor, a stereotypical
black's weapon, he cannot coldly slit Zack's throat. He
waits for Zack to awaken so that their ritual, which Lucas
conceives of as a duel, can run its course.

As the two men face each other, patterns of belief—
black against white and man-made against woman-
made—and the family's history and the men's own lives
juxtapose and condense. Lucas accuses Zack of looking at
him only through society's eyes, of brushing aside all his
ancestry, family, and past and regarding him only as a
"nigger."

> You knowed I wasn't afraid, because you knowed I was a
> McCaslin too and a man-made one. And you never thought
> that, because I am a McCaslin too, I wouldn't. You never even
> thought that, because I am a nigger too, I wouldn't dare. No.
> You thought that because I am a nigger I wouldn't even mind.
> (53)

Of course, Lucas sees that, murderer or duelist, he will be
slain in another societal ritual, a lynching. Yet when Zack
says, "Put down the razor," Lucas throws off the racial
stereotype by tossing the razor out the window and replies, "My nekkid hands will do. Now get the pistol under
your pillow." Zack says the pistol is in "that drawer yon-
der" (53). Neither will attack first, and Lucas explains
why: he has to overcome their relationships—"to beat old
Carothers" (54), as he puts it. So does Zack. Bit by bit
Lucas's passion rises. Calling Zack "white man" and so
resuming the role of black, Lucas tells him to get his pistol.
Zack rises, pushes the bed from the wall, takes the pistol
from its drawer, goes to the door, closes and locks it, and

tosses the pistol on the bed. "You on one side, me on the other," he says. "We'll kneel down and grip hands. We wont need to count." Society sanctions duels only between equals and therefore could not approve a duel between a white and a "black." Zack, however, is now compelling Lucas to become a duelist rather than a murderer. Lucas refuses. "Take your pistol. I'm coming," he says, trying to trick Zack into making the first move. Zack stays still but eggs Lucas on toward the duel. They kneel and grip hands, Lucas "facing across the bed and the pistol" the man with whom he had lived so long. Suddenly Lucas's eyes grow red "like the eyes of a bayed animal—a bear, a fox," and he cries, "Dont ask too much of me!" Their relationship is breaking apart. Zack thinks, *"I was wrong. I have gone too far"* (55). While that might mean "I shouldn't have made her my mistress," I believe that Zack is responding directly to Lucas's cry and means that drawing Lucas away from murder and into the duel has overstrained their relationship and is bringing about the violence that he has been seeking to prevent. Hoping to regain the pistol, he tries to grab it; and the two men grapple. When they find themselves stymied, "motionless, locked," Lucas sums up their struggle so far:

I give you your chance. . . . Then you laid here asleep with your door unlocked and give me mine. Then I throwed the razor away and give it back. And then you throwed it back at me. (56)

Lucas sees that they have been dueling all along; and when Zack admits it, Lucas breaks away and seizes the pistol. Instead of shooting Zack immediately, he checks the cartridges in the cylinder "Because I'll need two of them" (56). He plans to carry out a second ritual, suicide. Lucas's eyes flame again, and across the bed Zack, seeing Lucas blinded by his feelings, gathers himself to jump. Too late. Lucas is looking at him again. Still Lucas doesn't shoot; instead he muses on the family. He imagines, incor-

rectly, that Cass had persuaded Ike to surrender the
McCaslin land because the man-made McCaslin should
protect the weaker, woman-made one. Lucas thinks that
Zack has trusted in some such view for his own protec-
tion. Lucas is looking forward to vengeance, he says, even
if his own blood must flow, even if he must kill himself or
be lynched. On thinking of his own death, he suddenly
conceives another plan: "say I dont even use this first
bullet at all, say I just uses the last one." Suicide, as he
sees it, would be the perfect vengeance. Because it would
not betray the family relationship, it would "beat old
Carothers"; and it would beat Zack by leaving him "something to think about now and then" (57). His suicide
would also have a public significance far beyond a murder's or even a duel's. If a black man were to kill himself
with a white man's gun in the white man's bedroom, the
deed would set people wondering. As Lucas might know
but as the first-time reader cannot, Eunice's suicide did
just that. With Lucas threatening him, Zack might have
been wise to gamble on jumping him; but once Lucas is
considering suicide, Zack might be expected to relax. Yet
Zack too feels the ties of their ancestry and their youth,
and so he jumps. They struggle. Lucas jams the pistol
against Zack's side, pulls the trigger, and thus beats Zack
and Carothers. The misfire, though, beats Lucas, and the
duel has ended with honor all around.

The narrative then abruptly shifts in time, scene, and
tone. The temporal shift is almost subliminal. A single
sentence leaps into the future and looks back on the summer of 1898: "That had been a good year, though late in
beginning after the rains and flood: the year of the long
summer." The summer foreshadowed the season that
Lucas was entering, the long peace after trial. With the
phrase *this year* the next sentence returns to 1898, and the
narrative moves outdoors and grows calm. While Molly
tends Zack's baby, Roth, and their own baby, Henry,
Lucas is plowing. He feels at one with the land and with
himself. Plowing the soil peacefully is a contrast here in

the narrative with the violent digging undertaken in the main plots of "The Fire and the Hearth." Farming seems as natural a way to use the land as hunting and camping did when Lucas and Zack were boys. Burying a still and digging for treasure, on the other hand, seem unnatural enough to merit the Earth's jeering laughter. Resting in the noonday shade, Lucas muses on the cartridge that misfired. He feels that he has fulfilled the ritual roles of his heritage. By snapping open the razor in Zack's bedroom, Lucas had measured up as a black man defending a black woman and as a husband confronting his wife's seducer. As a man-made McCaslin he had thrown the razor away. As a white man, as a McCaslin, and as Zack's boyhood friend, he had entered the duel. As an animal bayed by the conflicts of his heritage he had grappled with Zack over the pistol, and as a black he had attempted to free himself of his white blood, his McCaslin blood, and would have waited for the lynchers. While recognizing his luck, he feels that he has lived up to his ancestry:

> *I would have waited for the rope, even the coal oil. I would have paid. So I reckon I aint got old Carothers' blood for nothing, after all. Old Carothers. . . . I needed him and he come and spoke for me.* (58)

His acts, however, certainly have not resolved all conflicts. Lucas still feels tensions between opposites—between men and women and between blacks and whites. Molly has not stopped tending to Roth and spending the nights at Zack's. "Impervious, tranquil, somehow serene," she is doing what she thinks right, but now with Lucas's acceptance:

> Nor was he any longer watching her. He breathed slow and quiet. *Women,* he thought. *Women. I wont never know. I dont want to. I ruther never to know than to find out later I have been fooled.*

Lucas still feels the centrifugal forces of sex and race:

"How to God," [Lucas] said, "can a black man ask a white
man to please not lay down with his black wife? And even if
he could ask it, how to God can the white man promise he
wont?"(59)

Yet the fire still burns on their hearth: the center of their
world still holds. The story of the confrontation, then, has
proved to be another archetypal romance: Lucas has re-
gained the honor he feared he had lost. And the romance
is once again comic. If he had fled in anger or in shame
instead of seeking confrontation, he would have broken
his family ties. Yet in slaying Zack, Lucas would also have
shattered his family. He would have been slain, Molly
would have been a widow, and Zack's son an orphan. So
the narrative is comic because it restores the society, the
relationships among the Beauchamps and the Edmondses.

Parts 3 and 4 conclude chapter 1 by carrying the moonshining plot swiftly to its end through a series of rituals.
Lucas and Roth play out a game full of bluffs. Lucas wants
Roth to report the still since the sheriff may believe only a
white man; and since Roth will suspect trickery, Lucas
assumes a role designed to fool him, the role of "nigger."
Despite Lucas's "enveloping himself in an aura of timeless
and stupid impassivity" (60) Roth doesn't regard him as a
defender of the alcohol tax laws but guesses that Lucas
wants to protect Nat's suitor. Trying not to be outfoxed,
Roth calls the sheriff. Raiding the still just as Lucas
foresees, the sheriff and his men sniff out moonshine like
hunting dogs. There are the arrests, the arraignments, and
the hearing, an occasion for which the county gathers.
This last social ritual disappoints the crowd because Nat's
and George's wedding, a family ritual, prevents the de-
fendants from having to testify against each other, and so
the charges must be thrown out. (Lucas's reputation and
the commissioner's boyhood hunting with Zack and Lucas
may have contributed to the dropping of charges.) The
marriage, which probably took place on Nat's Vicksburg

trip just after the arraignment, was preceded by the ritual of bargaining. Nat refused to marry unless Lucas would pay for renovating George's house. If she did not marry, her testimony and George's would be admissible. She had her father between a rock and a hard place, and he gave in.

Although the moonshining plot has ended, the treasure-hunting plot hasn't. Motifs likewise remain unresolved in chapter 1. In the opposition between sexes Nat has succeeded in marrying George and getting money from Lucas. On the other hand, George has bought a still with the money Nat got for their house; and although Lucas had disregarded Molly's admonition that the earth is "crying to get planted" (62), at the end of the chapter he is watching his corn and cotton springing up. In the opposition between ages the young people, Nat and George and Roth, have won some skirmishes but have ultimately surrendered to the elder Lucas. In the opposition between races the black and white have given way to Lucas, whose heritage combines them both.

The family history, too, has left issues unsettled. One has to do with possessing land. For first-time readers the paradox of Lucas's owning and not owning his field still stands; indeed, the section has twice reinforced it. The narrative has said that "it was not Lucas who paid taxes insurance and interest or owned anything which had to be kept ditched drained fenced and fertilized" (59) and has quoted Lucas's cavalier response to hearing that Roth had ordered Lucas and George off the place by sundown: Lucas told Molly, "You wait to start worrying about where we will move to when Roth Edmonds starts to worrying about why we aint gone" (76). It is not until chapter 3 that the first-time reader learns that when Lucas married Molly, Cass "built a house for them and allotted Lucas a specific acreage to be farmed as he saw fit as long as he lived or remained on the place" (110).

That issue leads straight into the second: the odd relationship between Lucas and Roth. The first-time reader knows by now some reasons why Roth might tolerate Lucas's being uppity. Lucas's wife had been Roth's wet nurse, and Lucas had lived on the farm since Cass's time. Only the re-reader knows the most important reason: Lucas is Roth's blood relative as Turl was Buck's and Buddy's. Yet nothing the reader knows so far seems to account for Roth's respect for Lucas:

> [Roth] thought, and not for the first time: *I am not only looking at a face older than mine and which has seen and winnowed more, but at a man most of whose blood was pure ten thousand years when my own anonymous beginnings became mixed enough to produce me.* (71)

Roth, of course, honors age and experience, but he seems to have gotten the Southern convention about "pure blood" backwards. In that convention the blood of whites is pure. Knowing that Lucas is a McCaslin does not sweep away the confusion because it is Lucas, not Roth, whose blood would be mixed. Roth respects the ten thousand years of purity in *most* of Lucas's blood; and since Lucas is ten-sixteenths black (or maybe nine-sixteenths if his great-grandmother Eunice was partly white, as Ike thinks [271]) it must be Lucas's black heritage that Roth venerates. This attitude is strange in a Southern white, maybe in any white, and becomes still stranger when combined with the odd way in which he and Lucas hold the land. Thus chapter 1 of "The Fire and the Hearth" ends without solving these puzzling issues.

While chapter 1 established many patterns, plot is the main pattern of chapter 2. Lucas outwits Roth and the traveling salesman and acquires the divining machine without risking his own money. That action, complete in itself as the chapter's plot, advances the treasure-hunting plot of "The Fire and the Hearth."

Rituals of hunting, gambling, and possession support the chapter's plot. The salesman hopes to sell Lucas the machine for the hunt. Trading would normally precede the treasure hunt, but Lucas entangles trading and hunting so much that in the end he and the salesman have traded roles, Lucas renting the machine and the salesman lugging it across the fields in the dark. The salesman, who expected to make a profit, takes a loss instead when he sells Lucas the machine for the buried fifty dollars and a chance to hunt treasure. Roth undertakes the mule hunt because he applied the wrong hunting ritual. He "expected to find the marks where the mule had been loaded into a waiting truck; whereupon he would return home and telephone to the sheriff in Jefferson and to the Memphis police to watch the horse-and-mule markets tomorrow" (84). Lucas and the salesman follow the ritual of treasure hunting with Lucas arranging for the salesman to engage in a variation: the salted mine.

In the rituals of gambling and possession, as Roth and the salesman find out, a man who competes with Lucas, like a man who plays poker with Buddy, "aint gambling." Without a down payment Lucas had persuaded the home office to send down the salesman and the machine. When Roth won't advance any money and the salesman won't go halves, Lucas swaps Roth's mule; and after Roth reclaims it, Lucas's salted mine gulls the salesman. When he and Lucas negotiate, they bet, bluff, raise, and call with the machine, the mule, the bill of sale, the imaginary treasure, and the salted mine as chips.

Chapter 2 is an episode in the comic romance of "The Fire and the Hearth." For his quest the knight must arm himself with, say, an irresistible lance; Lucas needs the machine. The knight goes through trials to test his spirit; and Lucas, undaunted when he finds no gold the first night and when Roth exposes the swap as a fraud, finally succeeds with the salted mine and obtains the machine.

Motifs play a lesser part in this chapter than in the first. There, like a current, they swept the action along, controlling the duel, for example. Here they merely eddy, gently influencing the two plots. Continuing to overcome Roth, Lucas also dominates the salesman from the start, "black-

and-white" triumphing over white, elder over younger, and McCaslin over commoner again. On seeing the sales-man hunker down, Lucas, a true countryman, perceives him to be only a bogus city slicker. The mud of the treas-ure hunt finally makes the salesman dress like the good old boy he is. When Roth is refusing to lend Lucas money, Lucas looks at him with "an infinite, almost Jehovah-like patience, as if he were contemplating the antics of a lunatic child" (80). Appearing only briefly here, the motifs of opposition, city/country and God/man, will have larger roles later in the book.

Prepared in chapter 2 for his quest, Lucas abandons it in chapter 3. That act forms both the plot of the chapter and the climax of "The Fire and the Hearth." Molly opposes Lucas's ritual of treasure hunting with other rituals. She threatens to divorce him and so to destroy their family by extinguishing the fire on the hearth. The act would be so dramatic a family and social ritual that it brings Lucas to his senses. She also tries to shame him by going treasure hunting herself. As she thinks him too old for such foolishness, so she hopes that he will see her as violating the conventional separation between sexes. At last, to pre-serve their family, Lucas relinquishes the hunt. Thus in the story's archetypal pattern of comic romance the queen to whom the knight owes fealty has commanded him in God's name to abandon the quest, throw away his lance, come home to the castle, tend his fields, and sit by the fire. The archetypal pattern and the plot of "The Fire and the Hearth" are now complete.

To account for the plot, however, is almost useless in understanding what "The Fire and the Hearth" means. At the core of its pattern of action lies not mere plot but family history. This history manifests itself in a disjointed and cloudy way. It must be abstracted from a narrative whose fabula has been severely deformed. The order of the fabula (1-17) is narrated in the order 9, 11, 6, 8, 12, 10, 7, 13, 14, 2, 15, 4, 1, 3, 5, 16, 17. Here is an outline of the fabula:

Fabula of "The Fire and the Hearth"

Date	Acts	Position in Narrative	
early 1850s	Buck's and Buddy's scheme for manumission	9 pp. 105–6	chap. 3
after 1869	Buck and Buddy dead. Ike relinquishes land.	11 p. 106	chap. 3
1874	Lucas Beauchamp born.	6 p. 105	chap. 3
ca. 1885	James Beauchamp runs away across the Ohio.	8 p. 105	chap. 3
ca. 1885	Ike searches futilely for James.	12 pp. 106–7	chap. 3
after 1887	Turl dead.	10 p. 106	chap. 3
1890	Fonsiba married. Moves to Arkansas.	7 p. 105	chap. 3
1890	Ike sets up a trust fund for her.	13 p. 107	chap. 3
1895–98	Lucas comes for his share of the legacy, banks it, marries, and begins farming. Cass dead.	14 p. 107–10	chap. 3
1898	Zack married. Roth born. Lucas and Zack in dispute over Molly.	2 pp. 45–59	chap. 1
1906 and after	Roth as a boy playing with Henry. Roth gradually learns about the relationships between Zack and Lucas.	15 pp. 110–16	chap. 3
Oct. 1940	Ostensible date of Nat's and George's marriage, according to certificate. (This may be a fraud. They were probably married on the trip to Vicksburg just after the arrest. If so, this would come in the first item dated 1941 below.)	4 pp. 70–2	chap. 1
After March 1941	Lucas hiding still. Avalanche. Finds coin. Nat watches him. Lucas goes to tell Roth about George.	1 pp. 33–45	chap. 1
1941	Lucas informs Roth. The still is found on his porch. Arrest. (See entry for Oct. 1940, above.) Marriage certificate revealed. Charges dismissed. George buys a new still. Lucas will supervise its operation.	3 pp. 59–77	chap. 1
1941	Lucas, the salesman, and the metal-detector. Molly wants a divorce.	5 pp. 78–104	chap. 2

Date	Acts	Position in Narrative
1941	Roth muses on his relationship to Lucas, on the still, and on the divorce.	16 pp. 116–18 chap. 3
1941	Lucas and Roth discuss the divorce. Molly is missing and found. Court hearing on divorce. Lucas gives up the search for treasure and gives Roth the machine.	17 pp. 118–31 chap. 3

Chapter 3 contains all the events dated before 1898 and two others: the accounts of Roth's boyhood and his musing on his relationship with Lucas. Much of this history is narrated in duet. Roth's perceptions and attitudes are phrased by the third-person narrator, who this time merely reports rather than authenticates Roth's account of the family history. That account is neither accurate nor complete. Roth thinks that James Beauchamp ran away "before he became of age" and that the family "never heard from or of him again" (105). In "The Bear," however, Ike reads in a commissary ledger that James ran away on the night of his birthday (273), and in "Delta Autumn" Ike meets James's granddaughter (361). Roth believes that Buck and Buddy left Turl a legacy (105–6); Ike has seen the will by which Carothers himself bequeathed it (269). Roth regards Turl as Carothers's "negro son." Because he doesn't add "and grandson," he seems not to know what Ike and Cass knew: that Carothers, for whom Roth was named, had committed incest with his daughter. Roth has never learned why Ike relinquished the farm to Cass; "The Bear" presents their discussion at length.

Even the entrance of Ike's voice into the narrative chorus does not suffice to correct Roth's errors. To introduce Ike's voice, the narration recapitulates the opening of the book: "Isaac, 'Uncle Ike', childless" (106). While the narrative reports some perceptions that can only be Ike's, especially in the scene when Lucas comes to claim the legacy (108), Roth's errors still creep into the history. According to him, Ike went to Arkansas with Fonsiba and her husband and left a third of the legacy, from which she could draw three dollars a week (107). Actually, Ike had to trace Fonsiba to Arkansas, and the sum was payable monthly (277–81).

Despite these errors, mostly about matters of fact, Roth interprets the acts of the family's history and the motifs of its heritage with ruthless honesty, not even sparing himself. His account reveals the powerful tensions that occur when opposing patterns of action and meaning condense and densify within the family. In chapter 3 family history, rituals, and motifs become so intertwined that they must be separated from one another, named, and described. Then the ways in which the narrative juxtaposes and condenses them can be seen more easily.

In this part of the family history James, Fonsiba, Lucas, Roth, and Henry are born; Fonsiba, Ike, Lucas, and Zack marry; and Turl, Carothers, Buck, Buddy, Cass, and Zack's wife die. Birth, marriage, death, coming of age, and divorce—these are among the rituals of the family, the acts whose limits and purposes are conventions. The Beauchamps have their own rituals, too: they keep the fire burning on the hearth, and for a special treat Molly likes a bag of candy.

Society has also established rituals of possession, and the McCaslin history is filled with accounts of property. Cass gave Lucas a farm and supplies for life; Zack left Molly a house and an income for her lifetime. Turl had a legacy but never claimed it, and after his death one third of it went to Fonsiba and two thirds to Lucas. Ike inherited the farm from Buck but relinquished it to Cass, from whom it descended to Zack and then to Roth. Ike's wife left him her house, to which he never took title; and Lucas gave Roth the divining machine.

Finally, there are rituals of opposition. At the age of seven Roth upsets the innocent equality he has shared with Henry and assumes the superior position by making Henry sleep on a pallet beside the bed. Answering Molly's objection to the treasure hunt, Lucas asserts that wives must submit to their husbands: "I'm a man. . . . I'm the man here. I'm the one to say in my house . . ." (120). Molly

uses the rituals of treasure hunting and divorce to counter
Lucas. When, after trying to subordinate Henry, Roth
comes back to the Beauchamps' for dinner, they serve him
alone instead of dining with him. Thus they turn the family ritual of sharing meals into a ritual of opposition, a way
to show Roth how masters isolate themselves. Roth feels
the pain of that isolation; and when he cries, "Are you
ashamed to eat when I eat?" Henry drives home the point:
"I aint shamed of nobody. Not even me" (113–14). Roth
could not make either claim.

Motifs sometimes support and sometimes conflict with
the history and the rituals. The meaning of maintaining
the fire on the hearth is clear when the infant Roth centers
his life on the fire (110) or when, back in chapter 1, Lucas
almost flings a bucketful of water on the fire in his rage at
Molly for staying at Zack's. To preserve the fire means to
preserve the family; to destroy one would be to destroy
the other. Motif and ritual support one another; they are
condensed. On the other hand, Lucas is too old for treasure hunting. His age is juxtaposed to his act, motif to
ritual. As Molly says, "He dont look it, but he's sixty-
seven years old. And when a man that old takes up
money-hunting, it's like when he takes up gambling or
whisky or women. He aint going to have time to quit"
(103). Ike's age too conflicts with his acts. According to the
narrator, Ike was born old and has grown steadily
younger until, past seventy, "he had acquired something
of a young boy's high and selfless innocence" (106).

Most common of all are motifs that support and conflict
with rituals and with one another simultaneously. Thus
blood ties are motifs: they bind people together into a
family. Yet within the family the blood ties along with
other motifs—conventions of sex, race, age, and possession—divide them. Roth pays respect to Lucas as an elder
and a McCaslin; Lucas, who bows to no man, still has
regard for Roth as an Edmonds and a white. The land they
share unites them but embroils them in conflict. Lucas
ignores Roth's advice about farming, refuses to let a trac-

tor cross the land he owns in the middle of Roth's fields, forbids Roth's crop-dusters to fly overhead, and yet draws supplies from Roth's commissary without paying for them. Nevertheless, Lucas challenges Roth with "You aint got any complaints about the way I farm my land and make my crop, have you?" (120). Yet even though Lucas is the man in his house and is a man-made McCaslin, he finally gives way to his wife and the woman-made Roth, both also younger than Lucas. His desire for possessions, a trait inherited from Carothers, also gives way to even stronger forces that are becoming visible in "The Fire and the Hearth." At the beginning of the story the narrative names them "ancestors" and "conscience." There Roth gives Molly a small sack of candy. Although he would have called his gift a libation to his luck, the narrator contradicts him: "actually it was to his ancestors and to the conscience which he would have probably affirmed he did not possess, in the form, the person, of the negro woman . . ." (99). At the story's end Lucas also gives Molly candy. In that gift and in his submission to her he too pays homage to ancestors and conscience. To obey Molly has become such homage because of the way chapter 3 has reinterpreted her character and endowed her with meaning. The first two chapters portrayed her from Lucas's viewpoint. In her youth she seemed tranquil and serene but "impervious" (59), somehow insulated from and unsympathetic toward Lucas; now that she is old, Lucas regards her as frail, querulous, and lacking in discretion. In chapter 3, however, she speaks like a seer. Through her we hear the voice of the Earth and a new voice as well, the voice of God:

> He's doing a thing the Lord aint meant for folks to do. And I'm afraid. . . . I'm afraid he's going to find it. . . . Because God say, "What's rendered to My earth, it belong to Me unto I resurrect it. And let him or her touch it, and beware." (102)

Molly had been, as God and the Earth are, tranquil and impervious, but now she has delivered to Lucas her "final admonitory pat from the spirit of darkness and solitude, the old earth, perhaps the old ancestors themselves" (38). The term *ancestors* comes to carry a double meaning, referring on the one hand to the previous generations of the McCaslin family and on the other to the primeval generations of mankind. *Conscience* also makes a double reference—first to obedience to God and then to obedience to the Earth, to nature's roles and its cyclic patterns.

The juxtaposition of these voices, motifs, and patterns of action from "The Fire and the Hearth" and "Was" is beginning to condense into themes. The reading of "The Fire and the Hearth" is itself shaped like Lucas's acts. Readers, expecting to follow the plot of Lucas's struggle with George, shovel aside the family history in order to get on with the story. But as Lucas gives up hiding the still when he finds the coin, they too give up the first plot for another. The coin that started Lucas's quest has started theirs. Next, wondering about the outcome of the treasure hunt, they push through thickets of family history only to find that Lucas abandons the hunt and returns to his family, to Molly and Nat and even Roth and George, and to his heritage—his land, his farming, and the fire on his hearth. As Lucas returns to what he has undervalued, so the reader finds that "The Fire and the Hearth" is not about bootlegging and treasure hunting but about the family's history and heritage. At its core are not plots but motifs: the relationships of man and woman, black and white, McCaslin and Beauchamp and Edmonds, elder and younger, city and country, man and the earth, owning and not owning, crops on which sweat has fallen and treasure on which there is no sweat. In "The Fire and the Hearth" these motifs are juxtaposed to one another until they condense into theme.

The narrative overwhelms us with motifs and patterns of action. Beneath the complexity of their entanglement, however, lie simpler and more basic patterns that can bring order to that complexity. The motifs, as we have seen, are oppositions like black/white and man/woman.

Thus they fit the form X/Y ("X is opposed to Y"). In the patterns of action—ritual, plot, fabula, and history—act succeeds act. These patterns therefore take the form X → Y ("X leads to Y"). In itself X/Y is static. On the other hand, X → Y is linear and dynamic, the pattern of change. X → Y takes two forms: (X → Y) in which the action has determinate limits and (. . . X → Y . . .) in which the ends are unknown. The former is the pattern of ritual, plot, and fabula; the latter, the pattern of history.

Although each motif presents a set of opposites X/Y, the opposites cannot be stacked up with X's over X's and Y's over Y's like two neat piles of bricks. Instead they overlap, perhaps like bricks set at random in a wall. A simple diagram contrasting Molly, Lucas, and Roth illustrates the overlapping:

Motif	Molly ⟵⟶ Lucas		Lucas ⟷ Roth	
Sex	woman	man	man-made	woman-made
Family	wife	husband	cousin	cousin
Family	non-McCaslin	McCaslin	McCaslin	Edmonds
Age	younger	elder	elder	younger
Race	black	black-white	black-white	white
City/country	city	country		
God/man	God	man		
Owner/holder			holder	owner

By the time the reader adds Nat, George, Zack, and the salesman and works in the four plots and, say, the voices of God and the Earth, the tensions that stem from such overlapping are plain. These tensions are crucial as a source of unity in *Go Down, Moses*. The broader society, the South or the nation, may conventionally conceive of those oppositions as static contraries. Within the McCaslin family's heritage, however, the blood of blacks and whites runs in the veins of Tomey, Turl, James, Fonsiba, Lucas, Henry, and Nat. Family ties bind together the McCaslins, the Edmondses, and the Beauchamps even while oppositions of race, sex, possession, and so on drive them apart. This dynamic tension looks like a major theme of *Go Down, Moses*.

As the family's heritage of condensed motifs contributes to theme, so does the family's history, a series of acts in the form (. . . X → Y . . .), in which people who embody the motifs become more and more entangled with one another. The McCaslin history tells of entanglement, most obviously the entanglement of blacks and whites. No matter how racist the McCaslins seem—and are—they have often violated the conventional separation between the races. Carothers' sexual relations with slave women is not a good example. He may have violated convention but not custom. But in many later acts the McCaslins did break the conventions—that is, the family employed society's rituals (X → Y) in unconventional ways. Carothers left Turl a legacy, Buck and Buddy set up their scheme for manumission, and Ike tried to give James his legacy and tracked Fonsiba down to give her hers. Cass allotted land to Lucas, Lucas fought Zack, and Molly reared Roth. These uses of the rituals, along with the motifs, keep Roth, Molly, and Lucas irrevocably involved with one another through their history and their heritage.

In Roth the tensions and entanglements of heritage (X/Y) and history (X → Y) are dynamic. They seethe in him. Hearing Molly's complaint brings about "an abrupt boiling-over of an accumulation of floutings and outrages covering not only his span but his father's lifetime too, back into the time of his grandfather . . ." (104). The twenty years he has run the farm as Zack, Cass, and Carothers had done seems to him "one long and unbroken course of outrageous trouble and conflict . . . with the old negro who in his case did not even bother to remember not to call him mister, who called him Mr Edmonds and Mister Carothers or Carothers or Roth or son or spoke to him in a group of younger negroes, lumping them all together, as 'you boys' " (116).

Lucas, on the contrary, holds the tensions and entanglements static. Roth's voice and the narrator's combine to say of Lucas:

Yet it was not that Lucas made capital of his white or even his McCaslin blood, but the contrary. It was as if he were not only impervious to that blood, he was indifferent to it. He didn't even need to strive with it. He didn't even have to bother to defy it. He resisted it simply by being the composite of the two races which made him, simply by possessing it. Instead of being at once the battleground and victim of the two strains, he was a vessel, durable, ancestryless, nonconductive, in which the toxin and its anti stalemated one another, seetheless, unrumored in the outside air. (104)

Molly, who is no McCaslin, is free of the tensions and entanglements. Her certainty and singlemindedness make her the ground on which Roth and Lucas must stand. Even in middle age Roth regards her as his mother; for Lucas she sits at the center of things, at the fire on the hearth. As she embodies the Earth, her hand "gnarled . . . like a tiny clump of dried and blackened roots" (101), she lies like bedrock beneath history and heritage. As a prophet warning against the "curse of God" (122) she stands above them. By gifts of candy Roth and Lucas pay homage through Molly to ancestors and to conscience or, in broader terms, to the creations of the Earth and of God.

Our attention to "Was" and "The Fire and the Hearth" has led us to develop ways to analyze how we read *Go Down, Moses*. We have seen that the book's patterns of expression resemble voices in choral narration. Its patterns of action fit the dynamic form X → Y as either the unlimited (. . . X → Y . . .), the pattern of history, or the limited (X → Y), the pattern of ritual, plot, and fabula. Its patterns of meanings are motifs, which take the static form of juxtaposition X/Y, and themes, which are formed by the juxtaposition and condensation of all the patterns.

3 / "Pantaloon in Black"

In "Pantaloon in Black" the reader faces another story that resists integration into *Go Down, Moses*. Continuing no plot from earlier stories, "Pantaloon in Black" offers only two straightforward links to them. Rider leases his cabin from Roth and has imitated Lucas in building a fire on the hearth. Both links seem trivial. The difficulty of integrating *Go Down, Moses* again challenges readers' assumptions about how it might be unified. Olga Vickery, for example, expects a single "framework" in which each story is a "ritual hunt" (124). Consequently she speaks of "the grim, relentless tracking down of Rider" (125). Although *Go Down, Moses* certainly contains ritual hunts, Vickery is describing a narrative Faulkner never wrote. As *Go Down, Moses* says, the sheriff and his deputy find Rider "by the merest chance" (157) when they stop at his house. Although certain he has fled, they discover him asleep on his porch. When they wake him, he lets them arrest him without a fight. The Birdsongs, who lynch Rider, don't track him either. They simply take him from the jail. Warren Beck offers "Pantaloon in Black" high but vague praise for three qualities. First, its "view of postbellum Southern Negroes in a pure state economically subject to the white race but unvexed by miscegenation and able, while fate spares them, to create a completely private felicity" (370) seems to him "brilliant realism" (374). Next, it is "consonant with the artist's announced major theme . . . —'the relationship between white and negro races here' " (374), and finally it is a "tonal-thematic interpolation"—"brief, idyllic, and tragic"—(370) between the stories of Lucas and

Ike. While much that Beck says is plainly true, his assumptions about authorial intention and about realism may
have carried him too far. As my earlier discussion of the
book's genre indicated, Faulkner's views of what he was
doing conflicted with one another. In addition, race has
been only one of the important motifs of *Go Down, Moses,*
which so far has emphasized family, sex, and possession
as heavily as race. Beck's expectations about realism may
likewise lead him astray about the motif of possession.
Because he thinks of the story as realistic and knows that
blacks are economically oppressed, he assumes that Rider
must suffer from that oppression. Rider doesn't. In fact,
he is proud of his earnings and his newly remodeled
house and feels no economic oppression at all. The motif
of possession does not support that interpretation. Furthermore, to treat the story as realistic requires overlook-
ing, or at least underplaying, Rider's great size and
strength. Far from a typical black, he is, to put it simply, a
giant: he steps over a "three-strand wire fence without
even breaking his stride" (136) and hoists a massive log. A
reader who regards "Pantaloon in Black" as realistic will
also have trouble accounting for Rider's vision of Mannie.

The section's seeming realism results not from its subject but from its pattern of expression. In Part 1 the third-
person narrator serves as authenticator. The narration
conveys Rider's words but is never influenced by his dic-
tion. From universes of discourse entirely alien to Rider's
the narration imports figures of speech. It compares his
shovel to "the toy shovel a child plays with at the shore"
(135) and, when he drives it into the earth over Mannie's
coffin, to a javelin (136). "The Fire and the Hearth" made
Lucas's feelings explicit, often indirectly quoting his very
thoughts. Here the narration seldom enters Rider's consciousness and then only slightly, touching more on his
memories than on his current feelings or aims, both of
which must be inferred from his acts and his brief expressions. By thus distancing Rider, the objective narration
makes him seem realistic. It may even ennoble him insofar

as its failure to articulate his grief deepens it by rendering it inexpressible except through his acts.

The distancing also helps authenticate Rider's vision of Mannie. A subjective narration would have made the vision seem more like his fantasy and therefore less credible. Moreover, the voice of society, speaking through both a member of the sawmill gang and the objective narrator, gives credence to the vision by foretelling it.

> Then the other said what he had not intended to say, what he had never conceived of himself saying in circumstances like these, even though everybody knew it—. . . "You dont wants ter go back dar. She be wawkin yit." (136)

Even Rider's dog authenticates the vision and supports society's voice by fleeing and howling as folklore says dogs do in the presence of spirits.

Before the vision Rider is grief-stricken. His acts show that Mannie's death torments him; but although writhing in agony, he has no idea how to assuage his grief. The vision fixes in Rider's mind an aim and a pattern of action, a ritual for attaining that aim. On seeing Mannie's spirit, he feels no fear. He walks toward it; and as he walks, it starts to fade. "Wait," he begs, but it keeps on fading. "Den lemme go wid you, honey." He wishes to die, to commit suicide; but in that instant he feels an "insuperable barrier" between them, between his wish to go with her and the act of suicide. Mannie vanishes; Rider remains alive. His own power, "invincible for life" (141), precludes his killing himself. Because he cannot simply commit suicide, Rider begins risking greater and greater dangers. By patterns of action other than those of outright suicide, he strives to bring about his own death. He stops eating; he walks himself to exhaustion and, sleeping, snores "like someone engaged without arms in prolonged single combat" (142). He is struggling against his own life-force. At the sawmill his work briefly tempts him to forget. In unloading the logs, he thinks that he may no longer need "to invent to himself reasons for his breathing" (145). (There the narration enters probably most deeply into his present feelings though not at all into his own language.) As soon as he realizes that he cannot forget, he undertakes his most nearly suicidal act so far, the hoisting of the log. All work stops. Despite a workman's forebodings—"Hit's off de truck. . . . Only he aint gonter turn wid dat un. . . . And when he try to put hit back on de truck, hit gonter kill him" (146)—Rider lifts the log. Afterwards he walks away and goes to buy whiskey. Since the day is Monday rather than Saturday, the moonshiner expects him to want a pint but sells him a jug anyhow. Then the moonshiner sees trouble in Rider's eyes and wants to take the jug back. He says he will "give you that pint, give it to you. Then you get out of here." When Rider refuses, the moonshiner grabs the jug. Rider strikes him across the chest and threatens him with words that raise the motif of racial opposition. "Look out, white folks. Hit's mine. Ah done paid you." The moonshiner, still offering him his money, responds in the same language: "No you aint. Here's your money. Put that jug down, nigger." Rider, apparently believing that the moonshiner is riled up enough to kill him, says in a voice "quiet, gentle even, his face quiet save for the rapid blinking of the red eyes," "Hit's mine," and, "turning his back on the man and the gun both," walks on across and out of the clearing. The moonshiner lets him go unharmed (146–47).

Rider tries to drink himself into forgetting, and he thinks he has succeeded. When his uncle tells him that whiskey won't help and calls on him to come home, Rider says, "Hit done awready hope me. Ah'm awready home. Ah'm snakebit now and pizen cant hawm me" (148). Rider imagines that he has forgotten; he thinks that the whiskey, the snake's venom, has stalemated his grief, the poison. Rider's metaphor parallels one used to characterize Lucas in whom two racial strains, the "toxin and its anti," "stalemated one another, seetheless, unrumored in the outside air" (104). If one toxin cancels the other as

Rider hopes, the situation would also be parallel; but
whiskey will not stalemate his grief. For Rider there is no
antitoxin. For Lucas, however, there is. His world centers
itself on Molly, on the fire on the hearth, and on the land
he shares. Rider has lost Mannie, the fire on their hearth
has died, and he shares no land, his cabin being merely
rented. Lucas can find peace, but Rider's universe has
fallen apart. As planets exert gravitational force on one
another, so black men and women are joined by the power
of love. Between Rider and Mannie, Lucas and Molly, Nat
and George, and Tennie and Turl feelings run strong—
love, trust, familiarity, desire for dominance. Their marriages entangle all their passions. The marriages of whites,
on the contrary, have seemed cold and passionless. Buck
fled Sophonsiba, Zack's wife died and was promptly forgotten, and the deputy's wife is as responsive as a rock.
When Mannie dies, she sinks into the Earth and, like a
planet falling into the Sun, draws her satellite Rider in
with her. On her death Rider sees that his universe no
longer has a place for him. He admits to his aunt that
whiskey "aint done me no good" (150). She begs him to
pray, but Rider refuses and challenges God: "Efn He God,
He awready know hit. Awright. Hyar Ah is. Leff Him
come down hyar and do me some good" (150). Rider has
decided to seek death again. He goes to the sawmill where
Birdsong, the white night watchman with a pistol in his
hippocket, shoots dice every night with the black mill-
hands. Pounding on the door, Rider repeats the image
"Ah'm snakebit" but erases any ambiguity by adding "and
bound to die." He addresses them all as equals, "gam-
blers," until the white man calls him drunk and orders
him out. Then Rider slips into the role of "nigger" and
appeals to the man's greed: "Dass awright, boss-man. . . .
Ah aint drunk. Ah just cant wawk straight fer dis yar
money weighin me down" (152). As he probably expected, Rider finds the game crooked. He catches the
white man's hand and forces him to drop the loaded dice.
In exposing him, Rider is preternaturally calm—"his face

still fixed in the rigid and deadened smiling, his voice
equable, almost deferential" (153)—as he was in confronting the moonshiner. Rider releases the man's hand from
his grip. He is now commencing the duel Lucas en-
visioned with Zack: the razor against the pistol. But Rider
and Birdsong, bound by no family ties, are not courtly.
When the man reaches for his pistol, the life-force still
runs strong in Rider. In the excitement of the moment he
cannot stand still and die; he must fight. Before the pistol
can be drawn, Rider whips out his razor and cuts the
man's throat. At that point Part 1 of "Pantaloon in Black"
ends.

Part 2 opens with the colloquial voice of society and
again a pronoun without an antecedent: "After it was
over—it didn't take long. . . ." The objective narrator then
enters, reporting Rider's lynching, while the voice of
society shifts into a legalistic style:

> they found the prisoner on the following day, hanging from
> the bell-rope in a negro schoolhouse. . . , and the coroner . . .
> pronounced his verdict of death at the hands of a person or
> persons unknown. (154)

The narrator introduces the deputy sheriff who arrested
Rider, and the deputy immediately takes over most of the
narration, the objective narrator now being limited to
characterizing the deputy and his wife and reporting their
words. The deputy tries to treat Rider's story as a comic
tale like Cass's "Was." Of course, this time we readers
know too much to permit that. Even the distanced narration of Part 1 has made us understand that Rider wished to
die, and we feel his grief. At the other extreme is the
deputy's wife: she feels nothing. In between is the deputy,
tired and "a little hysterical" (154). He is puzzled, unable
to interpret the facts he has acquired. He too knows that
Rider's story isn't comic, but he has not figured out how to
treat it. For him it is a disturbing enigma. Why didn't
Rider act grief-stricken at the funeral? Why didn't he take

the day off? Why did he hoist the log? Why didn't he flee? Why did he rip off his jail cell door and then holler, "It's awright. Ah aint trying to git away" (158)? Why, when he was pinned down by the chain gang, was he both crying and laughing? Why did he say at that moment, "Hit look lack Ah just cant quit thinking"? The deputy asks his wife, "And what do you think of that?" (159). We could answer his questions. We know that even though the jailor won't shoot him, Rider has made his death inevitable. Birdsong's relatives will insure it; for as the deputy says, even if Rider had fled, "the simplest way to find him would be just to stay close behind them Birdsong boys" (156). Rider's lynching is his suicide, one ritual serving as the other for him as it would have for Lucas if he had slain Zack. These questions, which we can answer, torment the deputy; to his wife, however, they mean nothing. The wife, the deputy, and the reader thus form a spectrum of society's responses.

No voice within "Pantaloon in Black" fully expresses Rider's pain. Only the narrative as a whole does that, and only the reader hears it. Nor does any character, black or white, comprehend his grief. Those closest to him—his uncle, his fellow workers, and his aunt—show little more understanding than does the deputy. Yet Rider is far from isolated. As the narrative says twice, society "refrains" from looking at him; it gives him his privacy. Both blacks and whites sense that Rider is troubled and make allowances for him. Thus, though no one understands Rider, many try to. No matter how imperceptive the deputy is, his narrative voice is more impassioned than the cool voice of the third-person narrator. The puzzlement in the deputy's voice reveals that Rider's fate, although beyond the deputy's comprehension, has entagled him. That voice must then suggest more. It must show that, even outside the McCaslin family, whites can come to feel the dynamic tension of their involvement with blacks.

This reading of "Pantaloon in Black" has dealt with its

voices and rituals. The other patterns of action call for little explication. The plot consists of Rider's suicidal struggles that succeed when he is lynched. The deputy's feeble efforts to make this romance comic fail. His "Pantaloon" is black and wears mourning; the romance is touched with tragedy instead. The fabula of "Pantaloon in Black" has undergone deformation but not fragmentation. The plot follows the fabula except for glimpses into Rider's past and for the deputy's recapitulation. The narrative includes just enough dates to fit its events into the fabula of *Go Down, Moses*. "Pantaloon in Black" occurs in the time that is the present for the text—that is, in 1941. According to the book's fabula, Lucas was born in 1874; and by 1896, within a year after his twenty-first birthday, he and Molly had lit the fire on their hearth "on their wedding night . . . forty-five years ago" (138).

For critics of Faulkner's novels "Pantaloon in Black" has been the greatest stumbling block in the way of seeing the text as a novel rather than a collection. Cleanth Brooks, regarding *Go Down, Moses* as the chronicle of the McCaslins, finds "Pantaloon in Black" "not a necessary part" (257). Joseph W. Reed, Jr., wonders whether "the story has any place at all in this book" and suggests that, if it does, its relationship must be one of "contrast" (190-91). Lionel Trilling said that *Go Down, Moses* is, if "not exactly a novel, then at least a narrative which begins, develops, and concludes"—but he excluded "Pantaloon in Black" from even that degree of textual coherence (*The Nation* 154 [30 May 1942]: 632). Even an article entitled "The Unity of *Go Down, Moses*" declines to affirm its unity; instead the author, Stanley Tick, concedes that "Pantaloon in Black" "must be considered the unintegrated and therefore nonessential part of the structure" (*Twentieth Century Literature*, 8, no. 2 [July 1962]: 69). Marvin Klotz's "Procrustean Revision in Faulkner's *Go Down, Moses*" condemns all attempts to show that "Pantaloon in Black" should be read as part of the book:

Few attempt to defend the relevance of this story to the other
matter in *Go Down, Moses*. The grief, transfiguration, and
death of Rider after the death of his bride Mannie have nothing to do with the McCaslin-Beauchamp-Edmonds family.
Some critics, who feel obligated by Faulkner's wishes, try to
find thematic links—either some ritual hunt or white *vs.*
Negro, or Negro conjugal love *vs.* white conjugal love—
which bind the story to the so-called novel. Yet the story
gains no force from the context, and loses none outside the
context. Consequently, such justifications lead not to insight
but to critical excess. (*American Literature* [March 1965], p. 13)

Maybe so. Yet we have already found "Pantaloon in
Black" tied into *Go Down, Moses* by the voices of the third-
person narrator and of society, by the fabula, by the rituals
of suicide and gambling, by the pattern of archetypal romance, and by the themes of love and of the dynamic
tension between blacks and whites as well as by the obvious identity of scene, the McCaslin land. Even having
made all those links, I think that a still stronger case remains to be made, one that gets directly at the most important way in which *Go Down, Moses* is unified.

The links noted so far have run back toward the two
earlier stories, but "Pantaloon in Black" foreshadows the
later ones as well. It introduces the ritual of the vision and
the correlative motif of life-in-death. The ritual entails
warnings, ominous changes in atmosphere, frightened
animals, the manifestation itself, a confrontation, the dis-
appearance of the vision, and the contemplation of its
meaning. Rider receives warnings when he says he will go
home. His aunt's is the cryptic "You dont wants ter go
back dar by yoself," but a mill worker blurts it out: "You
dont wants ter go back dar. She be wawkin yit" (136). At
home Rider feels his life with Mannie compressed into
that moment and that room "until there was no space left
for air to breathe" (140). The hound runs out and begins to
howl. Mannie appears, Rider approaches, and the vision
fades away. Rider, having cried out to Mannie to wait or to
let him go with her, silently decides to die. In "The Old

People" Sam takes Ike into the forest to see the visionary deer. The main stages of the ritual are repeated. Sam warns Ike with "Hush" and "Wait." The wilderness ceases to breathe, and the spirit-deer appears. Sam salutes it, and it vanishes. Afterwards Ike discusses the vision with Cass.

As Sam's salute, "Oleh, Chief. Grandfather," (184) and as Ike's discussion with Cass indicate, the deer is a paternal earth-spirit. It combines motifs of the Earth and masculinity as Molly combined the Earth and femininity. Mannie also combines these motifs. When Rider shovels dirt onto her coffin, the Earth draws Mannie in, her grave seeming "to be rising of its own volition, not built up from above but thrusting visibly upward out of the earth itself" (135). Beneath the tracks of a week's traffic the Earth, the dust of Rider's road home, has kept her footprints "fixed and held," "vanished but not gone" (137). As the mill hand believes, Mannie is among the "dead who either will not or cannot quit the earth yet although the flesh they once lived in has been returned to it" (136). Molly and Mannie then are both linked to the Earth. In his old age Lucas learns that Molly is the center of his life; and so, however strong the other pressures, he finally succumbs to her gravitational force. At the story's end Molly is alive, the fire burns, and the center holds. Even though Rider is young and full of life, his world falls apart when Mannie dies. After her funeral no ties of family, society, race, religion, or property can hold him. Not even his own vigor can keep him alive. As Molly drew Lucas back to farming the land, Mannie seems to draw Rider toward the grave. Like the shards in the cemetery Mannie was, for others, "insignificant to sight"; no one comprehends Rider's grief. But for him she was, still like the shards, "fatal to touch" and "of a profound meaning . . . which," as the deputy shows, "no white man could have read" (135).

Rider's death prefigures the dying of the Bear and Sam Fathers in both ritual and motif. All three commit "ritual suicide." By that I mean that all three choose to die and employ others as the instruments of their destruction.

Rider stirs up the lynchers; the Bear as the spirit of the wilderness creates its own nemesis, the dog Lion; and Sam orders Boon to shoot him. All three create the occasions for their deaths. Rider causes his arrest and awaits the Birdsongs in jail; the Bear lets the dogs find its trail year after year; and Sam trains Lion to bay the Bear. All three ritual suicides exemplify the motifs of the Earth and of life-in-death. As the Earth, speaking through Mannie, calls Rider to his death, so the Earth calls the Bear and Sam, too. When Sam first sees Lion, Ike describes the "foreknowledge in Sam's face" and says that Sam is glad to see death coming. *"He had no children, no people, none of his blood anywhere above earth"* (215). And Sam and the Bear continue to exist after death, as the end of "The Bear" shows. The motif of life-in-death that runs through "Pantaloon in Black," "The Old People," and "The Bear" is a variation on the motif of time in "Was" and "The Fire and the Hearth." In those early stories the past does not die; its effects echo down the years. Here even the dead may not die, may not "quit the earth" (136).

The motif of life-in-death brings to the surface a problem with the analysis of juxtaposition and condensation at the end of chapter 2. There I said that motifs take the form of X/Y in which contraries oppose each other. The motif of life-in-death plainly violates that principle; for if the dead still live, the motif's paradigm would have to be X = Y. This equation is static like X/Y; and as X/Y is a paradigm of juxtaposition, so X = Y is one of condensation. The opposition between X/Y and X = Y helps account for the dynamic tensions in the first two stories. For example, Lucas is a McCaslin and not a McCaslin; he is black and not black. Buck and Buddy are identical twins, but Buddy wears an apron. Time and again the sections of *Go Down, Moses* have asserted both X = Y and X/Y. These oppositions are paradoxical.

The motif of life-in-death also entails a new pattern of action. The first two stories followed the linear patterns of plot, fabula, and ritual (X → Y) and of history(. . . X → Y

. . .). In "Pantaloon in Black" Mannie has died. The line of her life has ended. But the return of her spirit shapes not a line but a circle, not $X \to Y \to Z$ but $X \to Y \to X$, the circle of seasons and of myth, the serpent with its tail in its mouth. Spirits also live cyclically in the sections that follow "Pantaloon in Black." In "The Old People" the buck that young Ike had killed "still and forever leaped, the shaking gunbarrels coming constantly and forever steady at last, crashing and still out of his instant of immortality the buck sprang, forever immortal" (178); and in "The Bear" the spirits of Lion, Sam, and Old Ben continue the hunt, "the long challenge and the long chase, no heart to be driven and outraged, no flesh to be mauled and bled" (329). $X \to Y \to Z$ is the dynamic form of juxtaposition, and the new pattern $X \to Y \to X$ is the dynamic form of condensation. The seasonal nature of its cycle is clearest when "The Bear" describes Lion and Sam as free of earth, and as "myriad yet undiffused of every myriad part, leaf and twig and particle, air and sun and rain and dew and night, acorn oak and leaf and acorn again, dark and dawn and dark and dawn again in their immutable progression and, being myriad, one" (328–29).

Beneath the shifting and tangled narrative of *Go Down, Moses* we have now found a basic structure, one so simple that it can be diagramed on a grid.

	STATIC /	DYNAMIC
JUXTAPOSITION	X/Y	$X \to Y \to Z$ $\ldots X \to Y \to Z \ldots$
/ CONDENSATION	X = Y	$X \to Y \to X$

Across the top of the grid the contraries *static* and *dynamic* indicate the nature of the structures beneath them. X/Y ("X and Y are opposed") and X = Y ("X and Y are equivalent") are invariant, frozen, motionless, static. $X \to Y \to Z$ is the finite linear structure of change as ritual, plot, and fabula while . . . $X \to Y \to Z$ . . . is the infinite linear structure of history. The cyclic structure of change, the pattern of myth, is $X \to Y \to X$.

Along the lefthand side of the grid the terms *juxtaposition* and *condensation* likewise signify contraries and indicate the nature of the structures to their right. X/Y juxtaposes opposites, antitheses. $X \to Y \to Z$ justaposes states that can be seen as distinct in the linear sequence of change. Such states might be the events in a fabula or the stages of a ritual. Juxtaposition places elements side by side; they are adjacent, contiguous, but not equivalent. Condensation, on the other hand, makes elements equivalent. The equation $X = Y$ condenses X and Y and indicates that they are to be treated as identical units in the narrative. Thus, although life and death are opposed and Sam and Lion have died, they still live because "there was no death" (328). $X \to Y \to X$ is the cyclic sequence of change. It indicates that while X and Y are not equivalent, the repeated sequences of $X \to Y$ will be: "dark and dawn and dark and dawn again in their immutable progression and, being myriad, one" (329).

The narrative's terms *juxtaposition* and *condensation* match the terms *contiguity* and *equivalence* that Roman Jakobson uses in his essay "Two Aspects of Language: Metaphor and Metonymy." There he points out that juxtaposition is metonymic and condensation is metaphoric:

> The development of a discourse may take place along two different semantic lines: one topic may lead to another either through their similarity or through their contiguity. The metaphoric way would be the most appropriate term for the first case and the metonymic way for the second, since they find their most condensed expression in metaphor and metonymy respectively.—(*European Literary Theory and Practice*, p. 123)

What we have already seen in *Go Down, Moses* suggests that the analysis of its structure remains inadequate. The narrative is rich in juxtaposition and condensation and in the static and the dynamic. Faced with opposites, it refuses to accept one and reject the other. Instead, it affirms them both. In the narrative the static X/Y and $X = Y$ are at once true, and the dynamic relationships form simultaneously both the line $X \to Y \to Z$ and the circle $X \to Y \to X$. In affirming opposites, the narrative becomes paradoxical. Paradox is, I think, the deepest structure of *Go Down, Moses*.

The diagram must now be revised to add the two new points.

	STATIC /	DYNAMIC
PARADOX	X/Y and $X = Y$	$X \to Y \to Z$ and $X \to Y \to X$
JUXTAPOSITION	X/Y	$X \to Y \to Z$ $\ldots X \to Y \to Z \ldots$
CONDENSATION	$X = Y$	$X \to Y \to X$

In the diagram the term *paradox* indicates the narrative's affirmation of the two sets of opposites, static/dynamic and juxtaposition/condensation. *Paradox* also names the new sets of relationships under the heading *static/dynamic*. The narrative speaks of static relationships as both antitheses and equivalents and of dynamic relationships as both linear and cyclic. Such treatment is ultimately paradoxical.

Seeing *Go Down, Moses* as paradoxical enables us to clarify some effects that earlier seemed puzzling. In discussing "Was," I noted enigmas that resulted from the "superposition" of patterns of narration, action, and meaning. Now we can see beneath those patterns more general ones and beneath the vague act of "superposition" a more concrete one, the assertion of paradoxes. The structure of paradox permits the unresolved conflicts among narrative voices and the separation and yet union of motifs of race, sex, family, age, and so on. It permits thinking of chains of action as both linear and cyclic. Above all, the conception of *Go Down, Moses* as paradoxical explains why readers have searched for unity without finding it. By asserting that opposites are true at once, paradox both challenges and stymies the mind, both demands analysis and frustrates it. Paradox—impervious—fascinates.

4 / "The Old People"

"The Old People" adds a new setting to *Go Down, Moses*. The McCaslin land was the scene of the first three sections; the big woods will be in part the scene of the next three. In "The Old People," "The Bear," and "Delta Autumn" the hunts occur not on the tamed land but in the wilderness. Against this primeval background "The Old People" presents its plot. Each of the section's three parts tells of a separate action, and the three actions constitute the plot: Ike is initiated, has a mysterious vision, and is enlightened by Cass. The plot is simple and direct, and so are the patterns of narration. The voices of society and the family speak here and there, as when the choral narration lists the hunters, each with his societal epithet, and recapitulates Cass's relationship to Ike.

> Walter Ewell whose rifle never missed, and Major de Spain and old General Compson and the boy's cousin, McCaslin Edmonds, grandson of his father's sister, sixteen years his senior and, since both he and McCaslin were only children and the boy's father had been nearing seventy when he was born, more his brother than his cousin and more his father than either. (164)

The voice of the Indians can be heard in the telling of Ikkemotubbe's history. Boon's phrasing colors the narration once: "A man might be smarter, he admitted that, or richer (luckier, he called it) but not better born" (170). The main voices, however, are those of Ike and the third-person narrator. The narrator dominates, mostly speaking

straightforwardly; but in treating the wilderness, the objective voice uses a more rhetorical style. For example, it
describes the boy Ike as

> having brought with him, even from his brief first sojourn, an
> unforgettable sense of the big woods—not a quality danger-
> ous or particularly inimical, but profound, sentient, gigantic
> and brooding, amid which he had been permitted to go to
> and fro at will, unscathed, why he knew not, but dwarfed
> and, until he had drawn honorably blood worthy of being
> drawn, alien. (175–76)

In conveying Ike's "sense" of the woods, the narrative
uses vocabulary and embedding grammatical structures
that are as alien to the boy as the image of the seashore
was to Rider. The effects of the narration here are much
like the effects in "Pantaloon in Black": Ike's perceptions,
including his vision, are made explicit; they are authen-
ticated and possibly ennobled.

Despite the rhetoric the section seems to have more
depth than its plot and voices should be able to sustain. It
is the paradoxical patterns of action and meaning that
make "The Old People" unexpectedly rich.

The section's acts are, in the first place, rituals and
therefore fit the dynamic pattern of juxtaposition $X \to Y \to$
Z. Part 1 tells how Sam prepared Ike to kill the deer. This
is, of course, an account of an initiation ritual. It began
years back when Ike grew old enough to carry a shotgun
and Sam undertook to teach him "the woods, to hunt,
when to shoot and when not to shoot, when to kill and
when not to kill, and better, what to do with it afterward"
(170). With Sam standing behind his shoulder, the eight-
year-old Ike shot his first running rabbit; and by the time
Ike was nine, Sam declared, "I done taught you all there is
of this settled country. You can hunt it good as I can now.
You are ready for the Big Bottom now, for bear and deer.
Hunter's meat. Next year you will be ten. You will write
your age in two numbers and you will be ready to become

a man" (174). For three seasons in the Big Woods Sam takes Ike to the stands allotted to the boy and is at his shoulder when Ike sees his first running deer. "Now," Sam says paradoxically, "shoot quick, and slow." The deer falls, and Sam dips his hands in its blood and wipes them across Ike's face. When the other hunters come up, Cass asks, "Did he do all right, Sam?"; and by saying, "He done all right," Sam declares that Ike has been initiated as a hunter (163–65).

Parts 2 and 3 of "The Old People" present a ritual of the vision much like the one in "Pantaloon in Black." At first neither Sam nor Cass warns Ike about what to expect; but while Ike waits in the gathering dusk, the atmosphere changes:

> there was a condensing, a densifying, of what he had thought was the gray and unchanging light until he realised suddenly that it was his own breathing, his heart, his blood— something, all things. (182)

The wilderness itself ceases to breathe, "leaning, stooping overhead with its breath held, tremendous and impartial and waiting" (182). Then the atmosphere changes again. The wilderness seems to turn away from Ike; Walter Ewell fires his rifle and sounds his hunting horn. In dejection Ike has already lowered his rifle and started toward Ewell's stand when Sam, gazing steadily into the woods, warns him to hush and wait; and Ike looks up and sees the vi- sion, the buck "coming down the ridge, as if it were walk- ing out of the very sound of the horn which related its death"; and Sam, "standing beside the boy now" rather than behind him, speaks in the Indians' tongue, "Oleh, Chief. Grandfather" (184). After this manifestation in Part 2, Part 3 goes on to the last stage of the ritual of the vision: Cass, a hunter and Ike's elder, interprets the vision and thereby reveals that he too is an initiate.

To support and to modify the rituals, the narrative masses motifs. At each stage—the shot, the vision, and the enlightenment—Ike is paired with an elder. Thus the initiation inevitably calls up motifs of age, motifs that assign characters places in a hierarchy in which age is juxtaposed to age, X to Y. Ike is the youngest. To him Cass, sixteen years older, seems like a father. Ike looks up to the sixty-year-old Sam Fathers with awe; and although Cass is a grown man and owns the farm where Sam works, Sam bears himself toward Cass "as an older man to a younger" (170). Yet X is also equivalent to Y. At the climax of Ike's initiation, when he shoots the deer, he becomes a man; and as he does so, the narrative instantly ages him by leaping into the future: "The boy did not remember that shot at all. He would live to be eighty . . . , but he would never hear that shot . . ." (163). When the spirit-deer appears, Sam and Ike are standing side by side. The initiation has united them, the young and the old, in a sphere beyond age and time, a sphere defined by the paradoxical motif of life-in-death.

> They were the white boy, marked forever, and the old dark man . . . who had marked him . . . ; the hands, the touch, the first worthy blood which he had been found at last worthy to draw, joining him and the man forever, so that the man would continue to live past the boy's seventy years and then eighty years, long after the man himself had entered the earth. (165)

The initiation calls up, equally inevitably, the motif that distinguishes true hunters from hunters, nonhunters, and false hunters. The dogs that moil around Ike's deer are whipped back by Tennie's Jim and Boon Hogganbeck, a nonhunter and a false one. Jim, who first appeared in "Was," handles the dogs but never hunts. Boon hunts but with an incompetence that makes him the butt of jokes. When Boon says that he was so close to a deer that "If I'd a knowed he was there, I could have cut his throat with my pocket knife," Ewell replies, "Maybe that's why he run. He saw you never had your gun" (178–79). The initiation has transformed Ike from a nonhunter, a child who couldn't carry a gun, to a mere rabbit hunter, and then to a hunter, and finally to a true hunter, an initiate.

The ritual of the vision gains power from each of these motifs. In saying, "Oleh, Chief. Grandfather," Sam pays homage to his superior and his senior; and Cass interprets the vision in terms of both life-in-death and hunting:

> you always wear out life long before you have exhausted the possibilities of living. And all that must be somewhere. . . . the earth dont want to just keep things, hoard them; it wants to use them again. Look at the seed, the acorns, at what happens even to carrion when you try to bury it: it refuses too, seethes and struggles too . . . hunting the sun still. (186)

A motif that both juxtaposes and condenses darkness and light adds significance to the initiation and especially to the vision. The deer Ike killed materialized like a spirit in a vision of light:

> Then the buck was there. He did not come into sight; he was just there, looking not like a ghost but as if all of light were condensed in him and he were the source of it, not only moving in it but disseminating it. (163)

The central acts of the rituals—shooting the deer at dawn and seeing the vision at dusk—take place on the border between light and dark. Moments of contemplation and evaluation, on the other hand, occur beneath the stars. It is night when Sam talks of the Indians, the People; and he declares Ike ready for the Big Woods "under the high, fierce August stars" (174). Cass interprets the vision in the darkness "where the scoured and icy stars glittered" (186).

This enlightenment comes to only a few. Not even all the hunters experience that stage of the initiation. Sam has shown Cass and Ike the spirit-deer; but Walter Ewell, whose rifle never misses, is puzzled by the large tracks beside the little buck he shot. Through the initiation Ike realizes that men are not alone in the woods. To him, as to society at large, Jobaker once seemed isolated, consorting with "nobody," a word now revealed as a punning oxymoron. After Jobaker's death Sam moved into the woods, choosing a seeming isolation that Ike did not understand:

> "If Jobaker's dead like they say," he said, "and Sam hasn't got anybody but us at all kin to him, why does he want to go to the Big Bottom now . . . ?" (174)

After the first hunt, however, when Sam stays behind in the woods and Ike rides back to the farm with the other hunters, the narrative reverses the expected description of isolation by conveying Ike's feeling that he was "returning solitary and alone to the settled familiar land" (175). The narrative implies, and Ike senses, spirits not yet revealed; and Part 1 ends with an even clearer anticipation of the vision, for after the second hunt Sam returns "to what the boy believed, and thought that his cousin McCaslin believed, was his loneliness and solitude" (177). The initiation shows Ike that he is not alone in the wilderness. At the moment of his initiation and forever afterwards, Ike and Sam are paradoxically united in isolation; they are, in the text's oxymoron, "alone together" (178). Cass's interpretation of the vision reveals the life-in-death in which spirits seek the wilderness, the "places still unchanged." Men also want those places, Ike says, but "There is plenty of room for us and them too." Cass agrees, especially since "they dont have substance, cant cast a shadow" (187). As "The Old People" thus comes to its end, its two main rituals condense: the vision is a further stage of the initiation.

The vision and the enlightenment transform ritual into myth by revealing the cyclic nature of patterns that had seemed linear. Sam has initiated Ike into a mythic union with the true hunters, with the hunt itself as a seasonal ritual recurring every November, and with the old times preserved as life-in-death. Sam's stories have brought the past to life with Indians from the old times "actually walking in breath and air and casting an actual shadow on the earth they had not quitted" (171). Sam has also projected the present into the future so that Ike comes to see the cycles in which "the buck still and forever leaped, the shaking gun-barrels coming constantly and forever steady at last, crashing, and still out of his instant of immortality the buck sprang, forever immortal" (178). "The Old People" ends with a mythic revelation when Cass tells Ike of the duplicate vision; and that revelation, by joining linear rituals, turns them into cycles.

This mythic pattern of condensation is supported by motifs of equivalence, $X = Y$. The enlightenment that comes in darkness reveals the paradoxical, mythic union of opposites. Ike comes to "comprehend loving the life he spills" (181). The visionary deer unites the animal and the human, the chief and grandfather. A hunter's quarry, by being honorably slain, is preserved, its blood turned to spirit. Thus the dead, hunter and hunted, still live; and the past is eternally present, and therefore to be alone in the wilderness is not to be alone.

The rituals of "The Old People" have places not only in the larger cyclic pattern of myth but also, paradoxically, in the larger linear pattern of history. They are events in the book's fabula, in history's dynamic pattern of juxtaposition, $(\ldots X \to Y \to Z \ldots)$.

Fabula of "The Old People"

Date	Acts	Position in Narrative
1809–11	Sam Fathers born, the son of Ikkemotubbe and a quadroon slave. Before Sam's birth Ikkemotubbe has the quadroon marry one of his slaves. Two years later Ikkemotubbe sells all three to Carothers McCaslin.	2 pp. 165–66
ca. 1862	Sam takes Cass to see the visionary deer.	5 p. 187

Date	Acts	Position in Narrative
ca. 1874–79	Ike's view of Sam and Boon (1874–76). Cass speaks to Ike about Sam's life (1875). Sam moves to the woods in March 1877, after Jobaker's death. Ike's first hunt in the Big Woods (November 1877). His second and third in 1878 and 1879.	3 pp. 166–77
1879	Ike, 12, shoots his first deer and is initiated.	1 pp. 163–65
1879	Vision of the deer. Cass explains it.	4 pp. 177–87

Through the initiation and the vision Ike perceives the cyclic patterns of the life-in-death. Yet unlike the ritual hunts in which the buck forever leaps, the rituals here, the initiation and the vision, occur in time and can be dated and placed in the fabula. Thus those rituals ($X \rightarrow Y \rightarrow Z$) have places as acts in history (. . . $X \rightarrow Y \rightarrow Z$ . . .).

While the plot of "The Old People" centers on the hunting rituals of initiation and vision, the rituals and motifs of family and possession that we saw earlier in *Go Down, Moses* are also important in this section. Family relations and the ownership of both land and slaves are issues here as they were before, but in "The Old People" they concern not so much the McCaslins as Ikkemotubbe, not so much the white man as the Indian. According to Sam, Ikkemotubbe had carried out the ritual of expropriation. He had poisoned the eight-year-old son of his tribe's chief and forced him to abdicate. Instead of having inherited some kind of rightful title, Ikkemotubbe had seized the land. Yet he was not the first to claim tribal lands as his own. His "grandfathers had owned the land long before the white men ever saw it" (165). The expropriation invalidates Ikkemotubbe's claim to the land and therefore his right to sell it. Consequently Carothers could not have truly bought the land from him. Both Ikkemotubbe's and all the McCaslins' rights to the land are thus "as trivial and without reality as the now faded and archaic script in the chancery book in Jefferson which allocated it" to the McCaslins

(171). Nevertheless, since societal rituals govern the passage of titles from hand to hand, the land, even though expropriated, does pass from owner to owner. Ikkemotubbe does sell it, Carothers buys and bequeaths it, and heir after heir inherits it.

Yet the moral right to the land does not accompany the title. That explains why the McCaslin family's hold is "without reality," but it does not explain who retains moral possession despite the transfer of legal title. At this point, as at others before, the juxtapositions in motifs and rituals condense paradoxically into themes. The narrative begins its revelations about ownership as Sam conjures up the old times. His voice makes Ike feel like a guest on the land he believes "someday would be his own land." To Ike Sam seems to speak for the true owner of the land; he seems the "mouthpiece of the host" (171). But who is the host? It is the wilderness, personified time and again in the narrative. Before Ike kills the deer, the wilderness is "sentient, gigantic and brooding" (175) and seems to "lean, stooping a little, watching them and listening, not quite inimical because they were too small" (177). Afterwards it watches Ike but will never be inimical again (178); and before the vision it seems "to lean inward above them . . . tremendous, attentive, impartial and omniscient," and Ike thinks of the hunters and their quarries as being under the "eye of the ancient immortal Umpire" (181). This personification indicates who retains moral title to the wilderness. The wilderness owns itself. Men who think they possess it may pass papers from hand to hand, but the moral rights always remain with the land itself. No man can own more than a mere legal title to the land, just as no one can own more than a mere legal title to a slave. Morally, both the land and the slave own themselves. Their freedom is unalienable.

As umpire, in accordance with a ritual of opposition, the wilderness watches all who inhabit the land. It observes those who know how to follow the rules and those who don't, and it honors those who play the game well. They are the hunters, both the living ones and the Old People, "dead and vanished," who nevertheless seem to cast a shadow on the earth. Through Sam the wilderness has taught Ike its rules. He has learned that the land opposes ownership. As Cass puts it, "the earth dont want to just keep things, hoard them; it wants to use them again" (186). The initiation has qualified Ike to play at least that game, to live at least that life, with skill.

Insofar as "The Old People" is ritualistic and mythic, Sam is simply the mentor, the wise guide who trains the initiate in the ways of the wild. But by embedding those rituals in history as well as myth, the narrative engenders opposing forces. The line of history opposes the cycle of myth, and Sam's role becomes problematic when the narrative places him against the section's double scenes, the wilderness and the tamed land. Sam is the illegitimate son of the chief Ikkemotubbe and a slave woman. Ikkemotubbe had run away from his tribe as a young man; and when he returned, he brought the woman, a quadroon, from New Orleans. Before Sam's birth Ikkemotubbe married the woman to another slave of his. Regarding Sam as a slave, not as his own child, Ikkemotubbe sold him along with the couple to Carothers. Sam's history shows again that the Indians are guilty of an illegitimate expropriation, this time not of land but of people. Indians as well as whites have held blacks in slavery. In Sam's veins runs the blood of both the owner, Ikkemotubbe, and the owned, the woman. Thus in Sam the juxtaposition of owner and owned is condensed, and he himself becomes a paradox of possession. He is an owner even though he "owned so little that he could carry it" (175). At the same time he is the owned, first as a slave and then as a McCaslin dependent. Yet he is his own master on the farm as well as in the woods, with "no man . . . ever to say to him, 'I want this finished by sundown'" (168). In fact, Sam is to some extent the master of Boon, whose Indian heritage derives from no chieftain.

Sam's history brings in motifs of sex and race as well.

The paternal heritage is dominant. Boon's grandmother was an Indian; his grandfather, a white. Consequently Boon's blood has "run white" (170). In the woods the motif of sex assigns Sam a position: he is an Indian. The motif of race offers three positions in that setting, the roles of Indian, white, and black. The farm, however, has no conventional places for Indians; and Sam is therefore classified to a large extent, but not wholly, as a black. He "lived among the negroes . . . and dressed like them and talked like them and even went with them to the negro church now and then" (169–70). Yet he bears himself like an Indian: "he was still the son of that Chickasaw chief and the negroes knew it" (170). From the whites' viewpoint too he occupies an anomalous position. Unlike the McCaslins' former slaves he farms no allotted acres, nor does he work in the fields for day-wages like "younger and newer negroes." When he works, he does "white man's work" (169).

Sam's racial and familial relationships bear remarkable resemblances to those around Carothers. In "The Bear" Ike learns that Carothers had bought Eunice in New Orleans (267) and believes her to have been partly white (271). Carothers had her marry Thucydus before she gave birth to Carothers's illegitimate child, Tomey. Like Ikkemotubbe, Carothers treated Tomey as a slave rather than his child: he made her his mistress and fathered her son. The similarity of these relationships stands out in a diagram:

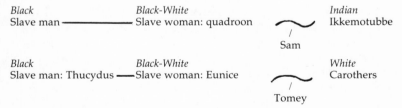

In Sam and in Tomey the heritage of races and of the owners and the owned combine. In them opposites join.

In Sam, at least, the union seems imprisoning and ultimately barren. Like Ike he fathers no children, and the
narrative throws some doubt on how close he is to the
wilderness. Sometimes his eyes, like Lucas's and Rider's,
give away the feelings he suppresses. Cass describes him
as an old lion or a bear who, having lived all his life in a
cage, suddenly smells something new. If it were the wild
land that he has never lived in, he probably knows "he
couldn't hold his own with it if he got back to it. But that's
not what he smells then. It was the cage he smelled. He
hadn't smelled the cage until that minute. Then the hot
sand or the brake blew into his nostrils and blew away,
and all he could smell was the cage. That's what makes his
eyes look like that." Sam's cage, as Cass says, "aint
McCaslins" (167); he is imprisoned by his heritage, by the
way the motifs of family, possession, and race are united
in his blood:

> he found out that he had been betrayed, the blood of the
> warriors and chiefs had been betrayed . . . through the black
> blood which his mother gave him. Not betrayed by the black
> blood and not wilfully betrayed by his mother, but betrayed
> by her all the same, who had bequeathed him not only the
> blood of slaves but even a little of the very blood which had
> enslaved it. (168)

In other words, the blood of white slave owners has betrayed Sam by tainting his heritage, by weakening his ties
to the wilderness, ties that run through the blood of blacks
as well as Indians. "When he was born," Cass says, "all
his blood on both sides, except the little white part, knew
things that had been tamed out of our blood so long ago
that we have not only forgotten them, we have to live
together in herds to protect ourselves from our own
sources" (167). Within Sam, as within Lucas, blood has
opposed blood. In Lucas the two strains stalemated one
another; in Sam the white blood of slave owners has
poisoned the rest. Lucas was not the "battleground and
victim of the two strains" (104), but Sam is "himself his

own battleground, the scene of his own vanquishment and the mausoleum of his defeat" (168). Readers expecting univocal meanings have underplayed such passages as these and have regarded Sam as the pure spirit of the wilderness. He is indeed close to the wilderness: he speaks for it. Yet he is paradoxically separate from it. Jobaker's independence shows by contrast how much Sam resembles the caged lion who never can be free. Jobaker's heritage is unmixed: he is a full-blooded Chickasaw who lives alone in the wilderness hunting and fishing while Sam lives on the farm and is supported by the Edmondses, for whom he sometimes works. Before Jobaker's death Sam goes to the woods when Cass takes him; after that death Sam feels that he must ask permission to move to the woods, permission that Cass naturally grants. Sam is less free than Jobaker, and of course Jobaker is not free either. He is isolated from his people and his time, "incredibly lost" (172) in the 1870s. Unlike, say, a wild animal, he is not independent of the human society around him but supports himself by hunting and fishing for market. In no man, then, do we find the freedom embodied in the spirit-deer, "its head high and the eye not proud and not haughty but just full and wild and unafraid" (184).

Ike's initiation, seen as an isolated ritual, appears to induct him into a mythic union with the true hunters and the old times by making him a participant in their cyclic pattern X → Y → X. But putting the ritual into the linear pattern of history casts another light on it. From the spirit-deer to Jobaker to Sam there has been a constant decline: neither of the two men is independent of society or at one with the wilderness as the deer is, and Sam is further from the wilderness than is Jobaker. Sam's separation undercuts his qualifications as Ike's mentor. His ritual may seem to initiate Ike into a barren and therefore dying fraternity whose primary existence is not in life but only in the life-in-death. Thus the narrative of "The Old People" takes two opposing stances. On the one hand, its patterns of action are linear and historical, its patterns of meaning mainly those of juxtaposition, and its theme one of loss. Before the white man came, Chickasaws greedy for power had already seized for their own the wilderness their tribe inhabited. Now white men have driven the Indians west; the last of the Old People are dying out. The lands they kept wild are now being cleared; the tamed land is spreading. History has left Sam no heir; and so to pass his Indian heritage on, he must convey it to white boys, initiating Cass and then Ike into a ritual that Ike will not be able to share fully with anyone after Sam dies. As an initiate Ike will be even more lost than Sam and Jobaker were.

On the other hand, the vision's patterns of action are cyclic and mythic; its patterns of meaning are those of equivalence, and its theme is preservation. Through the motif of life-in-death the narrative asserts the survival of the past. Though bodies may die, the ancient heritage still lives on in the spirits of the Old People, the true hunters, and their slain quarries in the mythic wilderness through which they roam.

The narrative, presenting these opposing views with equal force, thus assumes the stance of paradox. In "The Bear," the next section of *Go Down, Moses*, the assertion of both myth and history becomes even more forceful and compels both characters and readers to meet that paradox head-on.

5 / "The Bear"

Before examining "The Bear," it might be worthwhile to step back from the text to see where we are. Chapter 3 concluded the development of the full set of paradoxical patterns:

	STATIC /	DYNAMIC
PARADOX	X/Y and X = Y	$X \to Y \to Z$ and $X \to Y \to X$
JUXTAPOSITION / CONDENSATION	X/Y	$X \to Y \to Z$ $\ldots X \to Y \to Z \ldots$
	X = Y	$X \to Y \to X$

In chapter 4, which employed it first, I tried to make its use as straightforward as possible. Because the actions of "The Old People" lie closer to the surface than the meanings do, I chose the dynamic patterns of history and myth as the chapter's basic structure and treated the static patterns, the motifs, as supporting elements. That structure will not suffice for the greater complexities of "The Bear." No pattern of action is clear enough to serve as the skeleton of an analysis. We must now look at the plot, the fabula, and the rituals and see why that is so.

The plot is fairly simple on the surface. It contains five parts. The first leads up to Ike's seeing the Bear; the second, to Lion's baying it and the hunters' wounding it; and the third, to the deaths of the Bear, Lion, and Sam. Parts 1, 2, and 3 thus form a whole, the hunt. In Part 4 Ike and

Cass discuss Ike's plan to relinquish the farm, and in Part 5 Ike visits the place where Sam, Lion, and the Bear lie buried. To name the actions of the plot is easy, but it is hard to see how the last two parts fit together and how they are connected to the first three. Faulkner recognized the difficulty. A graduate student at the University of Virginia once asked him why he included Part 4 when printing "The Bear" as a short story. Explaining that his publisher hadn't been able to consult him when authorizing publication, Faulkner said, "That story was part of a novel. . . . If he had told me he was going to print it separately, I would have said, Take this out, this doesn't belong in this as a short story, it's a part of the novel but not part of the story" (*Faulkner at the University*, p. 273).

The fabula is too complex to provide a useful foundation for explicating "The Bear." Rather than clarifying anything else, the fabula itself calls for clarification; and the following outline attempts to provide it.

Fabula of "The Bear"

Date	Acts	Position in Narrative
1772	Carothers McCaslin born.	17 p. 266
1807	Eunice bought by Carothers McCaslin.	21 p. 267
1809	Eunice marries Thucydus.	22 p. 267
1810	Tomasina (Tomey) born to Eunice and Carothers although she is supposedly Thucydus's daughter.	27 p. 269
1832: Dec. 25	Eunice drowns herself.	23 p. 267
1833: June	Tomasina gives birth to Terrel (Turl) but dies in childbirth.	26 p. 269
June 21	"Drownd herself" entered in the ledger in Buddy's handwriting.	24 p. 267
June 23	"Who in hell ever heard of a niger drownding him self" in Buck's hand.	25 p. 267
Aug. 13	"Drownd herself" in Buddy's.	26 p. 267
1837: June 27	Carothers dies. Buck and Buddy free Roskus and Fibby, who refuse to leave.	18 p. 266

Date	Acts	Position in Narrative
June 27	Carothers's will leaves $1,000 to Terrel.	29 pp. 269–70
June 28	Thucydus refuses a ten-acre plot left him by the will. When Buck and Buddy offer him $200 instead, he refuses that too and says that he wants to "stay and work it out."	19 p. 266
	Buck and Buddy build a cabin, move from the big house, and use it as slave-quarters.	15 p. 262
1841	Thucydus, having assumed the name *McCaslin* and earned the $200, sets up as a blacksmith.	20 p. 267
1856	Buck and Buddy buy Percival Brownlee, the only slave they ever purchased.	16 pp. 263–65
1859	Buck wins Tennie in the poker game. She marries Terrel.	30 p. 271
	Tennie and Terrel have a son, Amodeus McCaslin Beauchamp, who dies within the year.	31 p. 271
1862	The logging train's first run. Boon, Ash, and the other hunters protect the little bear treed by the train.	62 pp. 319–20
	Percival Brownlee reappears on the farm as a revivalist.	44 p. 292
1862–63	A daughter, Callina, born to Tennie and Terrel, dies shortly after birth. Another child is born and dies.	32 p. 272
1864: Dec. 29	James Thucydus ("Tennie's Jim") Beauchamp born.	33 p. 272
1866	Brownlee reappears in Jefferson with an Army paymaster.	45 pp. 292–93
	Buck marries Sophonsiba. They clear the remaining Negroes from the big house and move in. Buddy stays in the cabin.	49 p. 301
1867	Ike born. Hubert Beauchamp presents his legacy to Ike, a silver cup filled with gold pieces.	50 pp. 300–301

Date	Acts	Position in Narrative
1867–ca. 1877	IOU's from Hubert replace coins and cup.	53 pp. 307–8
1869	Sophonsiba ("Fonsiba") Beauchamp born to Tennie and Terrel.	36 p. 273
1873–77	Ike waiting until he is old enough to hunt.	2 p. 194
1874	Buck and Buddy dead.	39 p. 281
	Lucas Beauchamp born to Tennie and Terrel	40 p. 281
ca. 1877	Hubert dead. Ike's mother dead. Ike declines to open his legacy from Hubert.	51 p. 306
1877: Nov.	Ike's first hunt: he enters his novitiate. Realizes that he will never shoot the Bear.	3 pp. 194–204
1878: June	Ike tracks and sees the Bear.	4 pp. 204–9
1879	Ike kills his first deer.	5 p. 209
	After Ike has killed his deer, Ash wants to go hunting. He sees and shoots at a small bear.	64 pp. 323–26
1880 or 1881, summer	The fyce attacks the bear and is saved by Ike.	6 pp. 211–12
	Cass and Ike discuss Keats and the Bear.	47 pp. 295–97
1881: June	Sam traps Lion.	7 pp. 212–20
Nov.	Sam has broken Lion, and Boon will tend to him.	8 p. 220
	Lion leads the pack.	10 pp. 222–24
1882: Nov.	Lion bays the Bear, and some hunters succeed in hitting it with their shots.	11 pp. 224–26
1882 & 1883, Nov.	Lion sleeps with Boon.	9 pp. 220–23
1883: Dec.	Ike's thoughts as the hunt begins.	1 pp. 191–94
	Boon and Ike go to Memphis. Boon kills the Bear. Sam collapses. Lion dies, and Sam is presumably slain.	12 pp. 226–64
	Ike takes down the ledgers and reads them.	14 pp. 261–82
1883–84, winter	Major de Spain plans to sell the Big Woods to the lumber company.	57 p. 315

Date	Acts	Position in Narrative
	General Compson and Walter Ewell think of incorporating a club and leasing hunting rights. They hope to induce de Spain to revoke his plan.	57 pp. 315–16
1884: Nov.	Ike, Cass, General Compson, Ewell, Boon, Jim, and Ash go on their last hunt together, not in the old woods but almost forty miles beyond.	58 p. 316
1885: Jan.	Boon appointed "town-marshall" at Hoke's, where he works for the lumber company.	60 pp. 316–17
June	De Spain sells timber rights. Ike leaves to visit the burial site.	59 pp. 316–17
	Ike takes the train into the woods.	61 pp. 317–19
	Ike rides in with Ash.	63 pp. 321–23
	Ike visits the site, sees the snake. Boon shouts at him from the gum tree.	65 pp. 326–31
Dec. 29	James Beauchamp runs away on his twenty-first birthday. Ike traces him to Jackson, Tenn., and loses him.	34 p. 273
1886: Jan. 12	After failing to find James, Ike returns to Cass the $1,000 legacy that Ike had gone to give to James.	35 p. 273
	Fonsiba Beauchamp marries.	37 pp. 274–76
	Ike takes her $1,000 to Arkansas where she has settled and deposits it as a trust in her name in a bank there.	38 pp. 276–81
	Brownlee is the proprietor of a New Orleans brothel.	46 p. 293
1888	On Ike's twenty-first birthday he opens Hubert's legacy and finds the coffeepot.	52 pp. 306–8
	Cass and Ike discuss the relinquishment of the farm.	13 pp. 254–61
	They continue the discussion.	43 pp. 282–95
	Again they continue it.	48 pp. 297–300
	Ike has repudiated and denied his inheritance.	41 p. 281

Date	Acts	Position in Narrative
ca. 1889	Ike marries, and his wife tries to make him take over the farm.	55 pp. 311–15
before 1895	Ike's wife has died. Lucas has claimed his legacy and James's.	42 pp. 281–82

The fabula of Parts 1, 2, and 3—that is, the items whose positions in the narrative are numbered 1 through 12—is as simple as the plot except for some recapitulation of Ike's initiation as a hunter. The fabula of Part 5—items 56 through 65—is also simple. Part 4, on the other hand, presents a fabula so lengthy and muddled that the reader has to struggle to get it straight. The existence of such a fabula demonstrates the historicity (. . . X → Y → Z . . .) of the narrative, but the fabula offers no clear-cut route through the text.

For the reader seeking a path toward coherence, rituals are more promising than the other patterns of action. "The Bear" adds to the ritual of Ike's initiation. He first joins the hunters in the quest for Old Ben. "He had already inherited then, without ever having seen it, the big old bear. . . . It ran in his knowledge before he ever saw it. It loomed and towered in his dreams . . ." (192–93). The Bear challenges them all, but it fascinates Ike. Step by step throughout Part 1 Ike is drawn toward it. With Sam as mentor Ike identifies the dogs' strange yapping as their baying on the Bear's trail. Sam tells Ike that the Bear was walking nearby, shows Ike its claw marks on the hound, and guides Ike to the Bear's footprint. But Ike is alone on his stand when he realizes first that the Bear is watching him and then that he is "holding the useless gun which he knew now he would never fire at it, now or ever" (203). At that moment, Ike passes beyond the hunters. He gives up their hunt and sets out on his own, whose form he cannot imagine. *"So I will have to see him,* he thought, without dread or even hope. *I will have to look at him"* (204).

The next summer Ike tries to track the Bear down. In three days of searching he sees not even a footprint. Then

Sam, from whom Ike thinks he has hidden his aim, star-
tles him by saying, "You aint looked right yet. . . . It's the
gun. . . . You will have to choose" (206). The next morning
Ike leaves his gun behind, an act the narrative defines as
"relinquishment":

> by his own will and relinquishment he had accepted not a
> gambit, not a choice, but a condition in which not only the
> bear's heretofore inviolable anonymity but all the ancient
> rules and balances of hunter and hunted had been abrogated.
> (207)

He has stepped outside the ritual of the hunt, crossed the
boundary dividing hunter from hunted, and now stands
in "new and alien country" (207) where his mentor is no
longer Sam but the Bear, no longer the hunter but the
hunted. He then discovers that Sam's instruction had not
sufficed:

> He had already relinquished . . . yet apparently that had not
> been enough, the leaving of the gun was not enough. He
> stood for a moment—a child, alien and lost in the green and
> soaring gloom of the markless wilderness. Then he relin-
> quished completely to it. It was the watch and the compass.
> He was still tainted. (208)

Relinquished and *tainted*—these words will echo in Part 4
where the narrative says that possession has tainted the
McCaslin land that Ike relinquishes. Here, carrying the
watch and the compass sets Ike apart from the Bear. By
relinquishing them, he hopes to cleanse himself of their
taint and be at one with the Bear. But he fails: he gets lost,
and even with the woodsman's skills Sam had taught him
Ike cannot find his own backtrack. At last, as Sam had told
him, he sits down—and sees the Bear's crooked print
filling with water. Heedless of any danger, he follows its
tracks, "keeping pace with them as they appeared before
him as though they were being shaped out of thin air just
one constant pace short of where he would lose them

forever and be lost forever himself" (209). Not "*or* be lost
forever." That would imply merely a fear of never finding
his way back to camp. The "and" expresses Ike's dedica-
tion to his aim. To lose the tracks and fail to see the Bear
would leave Ike lost forever, his highest goal unfulfilled.
The tracks, however, lead first to the compass and the
watch and only then to the Bear. By manifesting itself, the
Bear honors Ike's relinquishment and lets him succeed in
his quest. But by leading Ike back to the watch and the
compass, the Bear cancels the relinquishment, restores Ike
to civilization, and puts him in his place. Without watch
and compass Ike goes astray; relinquishment makes him
lose his way. Without the taint he is neither man nor
beast. Ike's effort to transform himself into an animal was
doomed. To share the alien country of the Bear would
require Ike to cross the gaps between himself and Sam,
between Sam and Jobaker, and between Jobaker and the
visionary deer. The Bear, by guiding him back to the compass and the watch, reveals the futility of relinquishment.
By guiding Ike back, the Bear also reinstitutes the hunt.
Unlike "The Old People," which focused on Ike's initiation and made the deer hunt a stage of the initiation ritual,
"The Bear" treats the hunt as an end in itself.

In presenting the hunt, "The Bear" accents the archetypal pattern of tragic romance that "Pantaloon in Black"
employed. The narrative calls the hunt a "pageant-rite"
(194) that occurs annually in November and December,
the season of "the year's death" (195). As a rite of the
dying year the bear hunt could be tragic only if the Bear
could die. In the fall of 1877, two years before Ike kills his
first deer, he loses his childhood belief in the Bear's immortality. Standing in the gloom of "winter's dying
afternoon," Ike sees the Bear's footprint, feels "his own
fragility and impotence against the timeless woods," and
realizes for the first time that the Bear is "a mortal animal"
(200–201). As the years pass, Ike tracks the Bear and kills
his first deer and the next year a small bear, but no hunter
can shoot the Bear because no dog can hold it at bay. In

the summer of 1881, however, Ike and Sam ambush the Bear, and their foolhardy fyce charges it. Dropping his gun, Ike catches the dog while the Bear towers over him "like a thunderclap" (211). The Bear has vanished without harming Ike when Sam comes up, lays the gun beside the boy, and says, "You've done seed him twice now, with a gun in your hands. This time you couldn't have missed him." Ike answers only, "You had the gun. Why didn't you shoot him?" Neither explains immediately his failure or refusal to shoot. Sam talks first to the fyce: "You's almost the one we wants. You just aint big enough. We aint got that one yet." And then when Sam says to Ike, "Somebody is going to, some day," Ike replies, "I know it. That's why it must be one of us. So it wont be until the last day. When even he dont want it to last any longer" (212). While the swampers who gather in hope of seeing Old Ben slain and even the hunters like Ewell and Compson continue to think of the chase as a hunt, Sam and Ike have a new conception. The yearly pageant-rites are nearing their end, the end of a cycle of life. The Bear is about to will its own death as a ritual suicide like Rider's. Sam and Ike foresee that they will have parts to play in that ritual. They think of the Bear's suicide as a tragic romance, a quest for death at the hands of others when life has no more to offer.

The stage is not yet set for the tragic action of ritual suicide. No nemesis confronts the Bear. Sam and Ike, the hunters who can track the Bear, will not slay it; and the hunters who would slay it cannot track it. They need— and in the summer of 1881 Sam finds—Lion, the wild mongrel whom he instantly recognizes as "the dog" (217). Once Sam has trained Lion for the chase, the roles in the coming drama have been filled. Lion is nemesis. Exhibiting not "petty malevolence" but "a cold and almost impersonal malignance like some natural force" (218), he "dont care about nothing or nobody" (220). Sam is the seer. When he first kneels over Lion's tracks while General Compson exclaims, "Good God, what a wolf!", Sam's

face, Ike sees, reveals "something." "It was neither exulta-
tion nor joy nor hope. Later, a man, the boy realised what
it had been. . . . It had been foreknowledge" (214–15). Like
the hunt itself the tragic action, the suicide, is a ritual
supervised, umpired, by the wilderness. Before the Bear,
a totem of the wilderness, can die, the wilderness itself
has to engender the nemesis. Sam, who owes allegiance to
the wilderness, serves its ends by readying Lion for the
hunt. By caring for Lion, Boon serves his chieftain Sam as
huntsman. Boon wields his knife in Lion's defense, slays
the Bear, and completes the ritual. Ike is the audience
watching the climax of the tragedy:

> It seemed to him that there was a fatality in it. It seemed to
> him that something, he didn't know what, was beginning;
> had already begun. It was like the last act on a set stage. It
> was the beginning of the end of something, he didn't know
> what except that he would not grieve. He would be humble
> and proud that he had been found worthy to be a part of it too
> or even just to see it too. (226)

Lion's part in the ritual is as suicidal as the Bear's. The
wounds he sustains while clinging to the Bear's throat kill
him. His task completed, he dies; and his body along with
the Bear's is restored to the wilderness from which they
came. Beyond these two ritual suicides there is of course
another: Sam's. In Lion's tracks Sam foresaw not only the
Bear's end but his own. Ike, when grown to manhood,
realizes that Sam

> *was glad. . . . He was old. He had no children, no people, none of his*
> *blood anywhere above earth that he would ever meet again. And even*
> *if he were to, he could not have touched it, spoken to it, because for*
> *seventy years now he had had to be a negro. It was almost over now*
> *and he was glad. (215)*

Sam's ritual suicide occurs offstage. Much of it may resemble the ritual of Jobaker's death and burial. Boon and Ike
have followed Sam's instructions: "He told us exactly how

to do it." Sam's body, wrapped in a blanket, rests on a platform of saplings. Boon says, "So we did it like he said, and I been sitting here ever since . . ." (253). How did Sam say to do it? Ever since what? Cass believes that Sam had had himself killed. Although Boon denies it, Ike refrains from supporting the denial and tells Cass only to leave Boon alone. Cass does not blame Boon. "I would have done it," Cass says, "if [Sam] had asked me to" (254).

Sam's ritual suicide thus parallels the Bear's. The Indians having been driven away by the white men's guns, and the wilderness now being driven back by the white men's axes, neither Sam nor the Bear has any longer a fit place in the world. The line of history continues, but their segments end, and there is no cycle to return them to their beginnings.

In Ike, however, they have a child. Although Buck died when Ike was about nine, Ike had had an abundance of parents, Cass and Sam as foster fathers and the Bear as his "alma mater" (210). Thus the narrative has raised but not yet answered the questions of whether Ike can inherit from Sam and the Bear and of what their bequest would be.

Analyzing patterns of action can take us only this far. While plot is too simple to unify the complexities of "The Bear," and fabula is too complex, ritual patterns run deep in Parts 1, 2, and 3. In the rituals of the hunt, the initiation, the tragic romance, and the suicide, we can see much of the structure of the three parts. Yet more and more insistently, acts raise questions of meaning. Rituals cannot be kept separate from motifs, and patterns of action and those of meaning insist upon condensing into theme upon theme. How does the narrative's conception of the action as tragic romance affect the meaning of the action? What does the narrative imply by presenting the Bear's death and Sam's as ritual suicide? What does Ike's initiation ultimately signify? With the deaths the hunt reaches its end as a tragic romance that culminates in ritual suicide. By conceiving the action as tragic romance, the narrative enno-

bles the Bear, the "epitome and apotheosis of the old wild
life" (193) and "old Priam" (194); and it endows Sam with
the stature of "the chief, the prince" (222), the seer, mentor, and the guide. As tragic romance the narrative also
asserts the loss of the heroic. No one who succeeds the
heroes of tragic romance can match them, and the
greatness of their times will shrink to the pettiness of our
own. As Wiglaf is no Beowulf and Fortinbras no Hamlet,
so Sam and the Bear will have no equal in Ike. He may be
good or at least well-meaning, but he will be no hero. Like
the romantic heroes who see that their time has run out,
the Bear and Sam accept or even choose their deaths. The
Bear dies as it had lived, in the chase. When Lion leaps for
its throat, the Bear catches him "in both arms, almost
loverlike" (240). This is the "last day" Ike had hoped for,
when even the Bear "dont want it to last any longer" (212).
Sam sees his own death in the Bear's and is glad. All in all,
then, by conceiving of the hunt as a tragic romance, the
narrative makes it trace the juxapositions along a linear
pattern of decline, $X \to Y \to Z$, and imbues the pattern with
meaning. The wilderness, embodied in the Bear and in
Sam, will not return; and Ike's fidelity to them will inevitably be fidelity to a cause that, however good it once was,
is now lost forever.

Still, the conclusion of the hunt is not so bleak as it has
sounded. Behind the linear pattern of decline, tragic romance sees a cyclic pattern in which losses are redeemed.
Death is not extinction. Mortally wounded, the Bear stag-
gers "toward the woods" (241), toward the source from
which it came. Sam begs, less of Cass than of the wilderness itself, "Let me out, master. Let me go home"
(245). From the gallery the dying Lion looks out "as
though to look at the woods for a moment before closing
his eyes again, to remember the woods or to see that they
were still there" (248). He dies with the day, at sundown;
and Boon buries him in the woods. Here the narrative just
hints that the Bear, the man, and the dog all "go home."
These hints are congruent with the motif of life-in-death

earlier in *Go Down, Moses,* and they foreshadow the book's major statement of that theme in Part 5 of "The Bear":

> there was no death, not Lion and not Sam: not held fast in earth but free in earth and not in earth but of earth, myriad yet undiffused of every myriad part, leaf and twig and particle, air and sun and rain and dew and night, acorn oak and leaf and acorn again, dark and dawn and dark and dawn again in their immutable progression and, being myriad, one: and Old Ben too, Old Ben too. (328–29)

That passage makes the cycle explicit and clearly connects it with the natural cycles of growth and decay and of daily and seasonal change. The cycle justifies the ritual suicides. They brought death when it was due. More important, the passage condenses juxtapositions. Although they look like straight lines leading through growth to death, they turn back to their beginnings. In the immutable progression of the cycle the myriad become one.

Even yet, though, the meaning of tragic romance is not fully explicit. In the course of the action exactly what has been lost, and what might fill its place? Does the narrative decry the destruction of the Big Woods and call for restoring the wilderness? What, in short, do these first three parts mean? Any answer depends on how we interpret Ike's initiation. It has taken him far beyond Cass and the other hunters, even beyond Sam. It has enabled him to go deep into the woods to see the Bear. It has barred him from killing the Bear but has readied him for watching it slain. In observing the denouement of the tragic romance, what does Ike see; what does he understand?

In his vision juxtapositions seem to stand out. The opening of "The Bear" appears to emphasize them—man against beast, aristocrat against plebeian, the tainted against the incorruptible:

> There was a man and a dog too this time. Two beasts, counting Old Ben, the bear, and two men, counting Boon Hoggan-beck, in whom some of the same blood ran which ran in Sam

Fathers, even though Boon's was a plebeian strain of it and only Sam and Old Ben and the mongrel Lion were taintless and incorruptible. (191)

The narrative pits the wilderness against men's claims to own it and uses the wilderness as a setting, not only juxtaposing hunters against quarries but also showing "the men . . . and the dogs and the bear and deer juxtaposed and reliefed against" the wilderness (191).

Yet the emphasis on juxtaposition is a false trail. The patterns of condensation reach the peak of their power in *Go Down, Moses* in "The Bear." The narrative signals, at first faintly but soon clearly, the importance of the patterns $X = Y$ and $X \to Y \to X$. The first of the many juxtapositions that condense in "The Bear" is the distinction between man and beast. The name "Old Ben" puts the Bear in a mediating class by giving it "a definite designation like a living man" (193), "a name such as a human man could have worn and not been sorry" (230). When a hound bitch gets clawed, Sam's remarks about her bravery bridge the gaps between man and beast and between masculine and feminine as well:

> Just like a man. . . . Just like folks. Put off as long as she could having to be brave, knowing all the time that sooner or later she would have to be brave once so she could keep on calling herself a dog. (199)

Although there are no women, males fill conventional female roles. Ash cooks and is "as deft in the house as a woman" (245). Boon kneels beside Lion, "feeling the bones and muscles, the power. It was as if Lion were a woman—or perhaps Boon was the woman. That was more like it . . ." (220). The Bear itself, "the old male bear," becomes Ike's foster-mother (210). The narrative exhausts the possibilities for condensing its three races: black, white, and Indian. Tennie's Jim combines black and white; Sam, black and Indian; and Boon, white and Indian .

The scene at the end of the hunt reveals both juxtaposition and condensation, both the line and the circle, both the myriad and the one. While Lion clings to the Bear's throat and the Bear claws Lion's belly, Boon leaps on the back of the Bear and drives a knife into its heart. "For an instant they almost resembled a piece of statuary." The dog, the Bear, and the man are momentarily frozen into a Laocoon. The bear falls and rises, Boon on its back again, his knife still probing for the heart.

> then the bear surged erect . . . it took two or three steps toward the woods on its hind feet as a man would have walked and crashed down. It didn't collapse, crumple. It fell all of a piece, as a tree falls, so that all three of them, man dog and bear, seemed to bounce once. (241)

By similes the narrative unites the bear with men and trees, the animal mediating between the human and the vegetative. The omission of punctuation in "man dog and bear" stresses their union, hunters and the hunted ultimately to be joined forever in the life-in-death.

Another kind of mediation is straddling. Once a doctor has assured Cass that Sam will get well, Cass plans to go home, leaving Boon and Jim to care for Sam. Ike, however, knows better. Sure that Sam will die, Ike refuses to leave; and finally General Compson overrules Cass and rebukes him with good-humored gruffness:

> You've got one foot straddled into a farm and the other foot straddled into a bank; you aint even got a good hand-hold where this boy was already an old man long before you damned Sartorises and Edmondses invented farms and banks to keep yourselves from having to find out what this boy was born knowing. (250)

Straddling is a way to bridge gaps between opposites and join them. Ike is a straddler too. Like Cass he has one foot into the farm since Cass is merely holding the farm until Ike is old enough to inherit it. Ike's other foot is obviously planted in the wilderness. The narrative thus sets up two juxtaposed standpoints, the wilderness and the bank, and a mediating position, the farm. *Bank* connotes the urban world that opposes the wilderness, and around the term other words and scenes congregate—*locomotive*, "townsmen" whose hunting clothes "had been on a store shelf yesterday" (224), and the train trip to Memphis where Ike sees that "it was not all right" and that Boon "should never have brought [his face] out of the woods at all" (231). The narrative might appear to separate the extremes completely. Trains, especially the lumber company train, would seem antagonistic toward the wilderness. Yet the narrative oddly uses the word *locomotive* in similes describing the Bear. Through the years the Bear has ravaged farms on the edge of the woods, leaving "a corridor of wreckage and destruction . . . through which sped, not fast but rather with the ruthless and irresistible deliberation of a locomotive, the shaggy tremendous shape" (193). The Bear damages not only the farms but the wilderness as well: "It rushed through rather than across the tangle of trunks and branches as a locomotive would" (211). With such similes the narrative condenses the extremes.

Ike's initiation has enabled him also to straddle the space between the farm and the wilderness, to learn to play "the best game of all" (192), the hunt. Here too juxtapositions—the basic roles, hunter and quarry—seem fixed but aren't. Hunters and quarries may play the game more or less skillfully. A hunter may be somebody who merely walks up game by accident but has a gun and knows how to shoot it. A dog may be a fool, and a quarry may be so easy to kill that it provides no challenge and must be protected, as Boon and Ash protect the little bear that climbs the sapling. To play the game more skillfully, hunters and quarries must learn to think like their opponents. Although Ewell, de Spain, and Compson drink the liquor in which "heart and brain and courage and wiliness and speed were concentrated and distilled" (192), they cannot fully anticipate the movements of the quarry. Sam and Ike, on the other hand, are able to kill bucks by waiting for them at their bedding-places and to ambush the Bear. The Bear, however, matches its skill against theirs. Each year it sizes up its opponents. Sam tells Ike that the Bear is "smart. That's how come he has lived this long. If he gets hemmed up and has got to pick out somebody to run over, he will pick out you" (201). The Bear then can think like its hunters. The roles of hunter and quarry thus condense. When the contest is most skillfully played, it pits hunters who anticipate the thoughts and acts of their quarries against quarries that think like men. In the best of the best game of all, the juxtaposed roles condense.

Sam teaches Ike the rules that enable Ike to stand on the boundary that separates hunter from quarry. Sam shows him how to condense the juxtapositions. Yet unlike Sam, who never breaks the rules, Ike tries to cast them aside along with his gun, watch, and compass. He tries to go beyond the condensation of roles that unite hunter and quarry in the hunt. He seeks to step out of his role, to stop taking part in the "ancient and unremitting contest" (192). But the rules are "immitigable" (192). Ike, who has gone from juxtaposition to condensation, is not permitted to pass beyond condensation to another form of juxtaposition. To do so would violate not only the rules of the wilderness, as the Bear proves by leading Ike back to his compass and his watch, but also those of the narrative. The narrative obeys rules that allow it first to juxtapose the assertions $X = Y$ and X/Y. It may then condense them into a paradox, but the rules seem to prohibit the subsequent rejection or reduction of the paradox to a simple assertion in the form $X = Y$ or X/Y once more. The narrative thus stands on paradox.

The paradoxes force us to confront the question of meaning in a most difficult form. What does the narrative mean by asserting paradoxes? Are such relationships static? At first glance stasis might seem necessary. By leading Ike back to his watch and his compass, the Bear reveals

that the hunt has a gravitational power that damps pertur-
bations in the orbits of hunter and quarry. While Ike never
returns to his original role as hunter of the Bear, he remains fixed in the field of the hunt, fascinated, watching
the Bear slain. But the Bear is slain. Its hunt ends and, by
ending, proves that stasis is not necessary.

Is stasis then at least desirable? Don't we want the
locomotive and the Bear, the hunt with hunter and
quarry, and the bank, the farm, and the wilderness? The
question is debatable. On the one hand, men kill the Bear
and "the old wild life which the little puny humans
swarmed and hacked at in a fury of abhorrence and fear"
(193). The lumber train keeps running, and men are felling
the timber of the wilderness. On the other hand, men
stand awed by the Bear and the Big Woods and hope and
expect them to be impervious to men whose attacks resemble those of mere "pygmies about the ankles of a
drowsing elephant" (193). In fact, the ritual of suicide implies that even those who die do not seek stasis. Sam and
the Bear die when they no longer want to live.

The analysis finally leads to this: whether stasis is desirable or not, it is impossible. In each relationship one of the
juxtaposed members cannot survive. The Bear, the
quarry, and the wilderness are doomed by the seemingly
inexorable force of history's linear pattern. Wilderness is
succeeded by farm, and farm by bank. Sam and even the
Bear know what Ike will not see: nobody can stand fast,
much less step backward, against the thrust of history.
They bow to the inevitable and find their fitting deaths.
For them the line ends. On another plane, in the life-in-
death, they will of course endure. There the cycle of the
hunt goes on. In abandoning watch and compass, Ike,
however, tries to move back from Y to X in the pattern of
history. The Bear has already refused to countenance that
effort, but to understand the full meaning of the Bear's
refusal and Ike's failure, we must grapple with Part 4 of
"The Bear."

For explicating Part 4, patterns of action fade into the

background because Part 4 is a discussion and therefore not so much a series of acts as a series of meanings. Since the death of Ike's parents, Cass has held the farm in trust. When Ike turns twenty-one, his coming of age forces him to decide whether to accept his inheritance or to relinquish the farm to Cass. As Part 4 opens, the two men are debating less about the act than about its meaning, less about whether Ike should relinquish his inheritance than about what relinquishment will signify. The wilderness has obviously helped shape Ike's choice. Yet the narrative turns away from that scene and places Ike and Cass "juxtaposed not against the wilderness but against the tamed land which was to have been his heritage" (254). Set off against the backdrop of the farm, the two men seem to put forward opposing conceptions. Cass offers a linear, historical view, tracing the legal history of Ike's inheritance back to the time when Carothers acquired the land. The line conforms to societal rules for transferring possession, for selling and buying and for bequeathing and inheriting. According to Cass, Carothers either bought the land or acquired squatter's rights to it. One way or the other he gained legal title to the land. From Carothers the land had been passed down properly, male heirs taking precedence over female, elder over younger.

> "You, the direct male descendant of him who saw the opportunity and took it, bought the land, took the land, got the land no matter how, held it to bequeath, no matter how, out of the old grant, the first patent, when it was a wilderness of wild beasts and wilder men, and cleared it, translated it into something to bequeath to his children. . . . Not only the male descendant but the only and last descendant in the male line and in the third generation, while I am not only four generations from old Carothers, I derived through a woman." (256)

Against Cass's historical view Ike juxtaposes his mythic one. Even though Ikkemotubbe took money for the land, he could not sell it nor could Carothers buy it because "on the instant when Ikkemotubbe discovered, realised, that he could sell it for money, on that instant it ceased ever to have been his forever, father to father to father, and the man who bought it bought nothing" (257). According to Ike, God

> made the earth first and peopled it with dumb creatures, and then He created man to be His overseer on the earth and to hold suzerainty over the earth and the animals on it in His name, not to hold for himself and his descendants inviolable title forever, generation after generation, to the oblongs and squares of the earth, but to hold the earth mutual and intact in the communal anonymity of brotherhood. (257)

Ike's conception thus begins with a mythic time in which all men hold the earth, share it like a family, like God's sons in the communal anonymity of brotherhood. For him the societal rituals, the laws and rules, of possession are illegitimate deviations from the primal state.

Cass counters Ike first by bluntly stating that Carothers nevertheless did own it and then by replacing Ike's static interpretation with a linear, historical view of the Bible's account: "And not the first. Not alone and not the first since, as your Authority states, man was dispossessed of Eden" (257). Cass sketches a "chronicle" that runs from those "sprung from Abraham" through the "sons of them who dispossessed Abraham," through the Roman Empire and "the next thousand years while men fought over the fragments of that collapse," and up to the discovery of the New World where Carothers bought this land (257–58). Why would God condone all that if it weren't His will? Cass challenges Ike to say whether God was "perverse, impotent, or blind: which?"

"Dispossessed," Ike answers. His reply makes God, in His being dispossessed, analogous to the Indians dispossessed of their communal lands by Ikkemotubbe's fathers and analogous to men dispossessed of Eden by the sins of their parents. Ike is reinterpreting the discovery of the New World. He sees it not simply as more land to be owned but as God's offering men a new chance to return to their primal and proper state. Out of the twilight of Western culture God led Europeans to "a new world where a nation of people could be founded in humility and pity and sufferance and pride of one to another" (258). Before white men first landed, Ike says, God "saw the land already accursed even as Ikkemotubbe and Ikkemotubbe's father old Issetibbeha and old Issetibbeha's fathers too held it, already tainted" by Indian chieftains who dispossessed their own people. Ike suggests that God let white men bring their corrupt concept of property into the New World to void the land for a time of the Indians' similar corruption "as doctors use fever to burn up fever." Perhaps, Ike says, God even foresaw that Carothers and his descendants would someday renounce ownership and "set at least some of His lowly people free" (259).

"The sons of Ham," Cass replies. His ironic response compels Ike to deal with the biblical text that society often used to support slavery. In the passage Noah curses Ham's son and condemns him to be "slave of slaves" to his "brothers" (Genesis 9:25). Ike replies:

> "There are some things He said in the Book, and some things reported of Him that He did not say. And I know what you will say now: That if truth is one thing to me and another thing to you, how will we choose which is truth? You dont need to choose. The heart already knows. He didn't have His Book written to be read by what must elect and choose, but by the heart, . . . by the doomed and lowly of the earth who have nothing else to read with but the heart." (260)

Although Cass protests a bit, he does not even try to refute Ike's rejection of that text. Cass will not try because he is juxtaposed along with Ike against the tamed land. Behind them both stand the shelves of ledgers, the farm's records, the history of the people who have lived on the tamed land. Neither Cass nor Ike glances at the ledgers. "They did not need to" (261); they knew the story the

pages told, a story whose meaning is crucial to understanding what relinquishment means to Ike and Cass.

The narrative of Part 4 begins that story, as *Go Down,
Moses* begins, with what seems a comic tale, the account of
the "anomaly" Percival Brownlee, the only slave Buck or
Buddy ever bought. Buck purchased him as a clerk only to
discover that Brownlee could not read and could write
only his name. Brownlee then claimed to be a ploughman;
and Buck, dubious, sent him to the field. When Brownlee
couldn't plough either, Buck assigned him to lead live-
stock to the creek since Brownlee "says he aims to be a
Precher." Buddy then noted, "Cant do that either Except
one at a Time Get shut of him." To Buck's "Who in hell
would buy him," Buddy responded, "Nobody . . . I never
said sell him Free him." Buck hoped to have Brownlee
earn his freedom; but when Brownlee caused the death of
a mule, Buck set him free. Brownlee refused to leave. Buck
asked plaintively, "What would father done," and Buddy
delivered his cryptic punchline: "Renamed him . . . Spin-
trius," a term for male prostitutes in Suetonius and in
Roman comedy (264–65). As the narrative of "Was"
stopped before revealing Buck's and Sophonsiba's marriage, the ledger entries break off before telling how
Brownlee left. After his departure, however, he reappears
from time to time in the family's history; and as he reappears, the ledgers reveal him as a pathetic figure who can
hardly find in society any place where he fits in. He crops
up as a revivalist and then as the homosexual companion
of a Yankee army paymaster and seems to end his career
as the proprietor of a select New Orleans brothel.

As the ledgers, like *Go Down, Moses* itself, grow more
serious, they become the source of the dominant patterns
of action and meaning in Part 4. They show rituals and
motifs of possession being transformed into rituals and
motifs of family. The ledgers, the farm's account books,
are records of property. Their pages are filled with the
"day-by-day accrument" (266) of debits and credits beneath short biographical entries, and even those entries

treat people as possessions. How was the property acquired? Brownlee was bought from "N. B. Forest at Cold Water 3 Mar 1856 $265. dolars" (264). Roskus was raised by Carothers's family in the Carolinas, Fibby was purchased there, and Thucydus was their child. What was the condition of the property? Brownlee depreciated rapidly, Roskus didn't know his age, and Fibby said she was fifty. What became of the property? Brownlee was freed. When Carothers died, Buck and Buddy freed Roskus and Fibby too. Yet, as the entries show, all these slaves force the McCaslins to see them as individuals. "One by one" in the pages of the ledgers "the slaves . . . took substance and even a sort of shadowy life with their passions and complexities too as page followed page and year year" (263–65). Each "possession" transformed itself into a person, and the ledgers reconstitute the existence of each of them. Brownlee becomes the "Son of a bitch" who won't leave. Roskus and Fibby also refuse to leave.

The ledgers go on to record not only the transformation into persons but also the further transformation into family:

Thucydus Roskus @ Fibby Son born in Callina 1779. Refused 10 acre peace fathers Will 28 Jun 1837 Refused Cash offer $200. dolars from A.@T. McCaslin 28 June 1837 Wants to stay and work it out (266)

Carothers's will left Thucydus ten acres of land, a legacy befitting a relative, although Thucydus is not related; but Thucydus refused both that bequest and the two hundred dollars offered him instead of the land. He stayed on the farm, purchased his freedom with his labor, and set up as a blacksmith in Jefferson. The next entries, in Buck's handwriting, form the enigmatic record of the actual entrance of blacks into the family. Carothers bought Eunice in 1807; she married Thucydus in 1809 and drowned in a creek on Christmas Day, 1832. On June 21, 1833, Buddy emended the last entry to "Drownd herself" and triggered Buck's

angry question, "Who in hell ever heard of a niger
drownding him self." Two months later Buddy replies
with curt finality, "Drownd herself."

The entries pose the puzzle that Ike asks himself: "But
why?" (267). Only when he is sixteen does that question
occur to him. Before, he had naively thought the ledgers
"fixed immutably, finished, unalterable, harmless" (268).
But now he is sixteen, old enough not only to ask the
question but to recognize the answer. Creeping secretly
into the commissary, he reads of Tomey's birth in 1810,
her giving birth to Turl and then dying in childbed six
months after her mother's suicide, and finally the mere
phrase "Fathers will." Ike understands the allusion. He
knows that Carothers left Turl the thousand-dollar legacy.
Ike judges Carothers's bequest with a mixture of contempt
and understanding. On the one hand, Ike sneers, *"I reckon
that was cheaper than saying My son to a nigger. . . . Even if My
son wasn't but just two words."* Here Ike does not quite see
how much Carothers has violated societal conventions of
possession by which the master's progeny by slave
women simply become slaves themselves, possessions
rather than heirs. In this, at least, Carothers is more ad-
mirable than Ikkemotubbe, who obeyed the convention in
treating his son Sam as property and selling him. By violating conventions, Carothers's legacy was "costlier" than
doing nothing at all. Even though posthumous, it was an
extraordinary act. On the other hand, in imagining
Carothers, Ike sees that there must have been *"Some sort of
love. Even what he would have called love: not just an
afternoon's or a night's spittoon"* (269–70). At this moment
Ike knows that he has not yet solved the puzzle, but he is
beginning to test a hypothesis: that Eunice committed
suicide because her daughter was having an affair with the
master. Ike sees the lonely man, aging and bored, sending
for the unmarried girl because he wanted "a young voice
and movement in the house." Eunice would agree, according to this hypothesis, because she would want her
daughter to be a house servant. After all, Thucydus and

his parents were not field hands but house servants whom
Carothers had inherited from his father, and Carothers
himself had traveled better than three hundred miles to
New Orleans "and bought the girl's mother as a wife
for. . . ." With the conception of the next word, not
Thucydus but the *himself* that Ike never speaks, his hypothesis collapses; and he sits frozen in horror.

> and that was all. The old frail pages seemed to turn of their
> own accord even while he thought *His own daughter His own
> daughter. No No Not even him* back to that one where the white
> man . . . who did not need another slave, had gone all the
> way to New Orleans and bought one. (270)

The ledgers conjure up a vision of Eunice's suicide. Ike
seems to "see her actually walking into the icy creek on
that Christmas day . . . , solitary, inflexible, griefless, cere-
monial, in formal and succinct repudiation of grief and
despair who had already had to repudiate belief and
hope" (271).

So the ledgers have fleshed out for Ike the lives of the
blacks who have lived on the McCaslin land. After that
vision

> He would never need look at the ledgers again nor did he; the
> yellowed pages in their fading and implacable succession
> were as much a part of his consciousness and would remain
> so forever, as the fact of his own nativity. (271)

In those pages he has seen "not only the general and
condoned injustice and its slow amortization but the
specific tragedy which had not been condoned and could
never be amortized" (266). As the blended voices of Ike
and the third-person narrator imply, Eunice's death is,
like the Bear's, the painful, inevitable, tragic consequence
of an irreversible line of acts. Her death resembles those of
Rider, Sam, Lion, and the Bear in being "griefless, ceremo-
nial." Her death in the icy creek is, like theirs, a suicide.

"Amortization" indicates another ritual, the gradual

payment of debts on which interest keeps accumulating. Injustice has put whites in debt to blacks; and the debt must be paid eventually, no matter how tolerant the creditor—and the longer the term, the greater the interest.

Cass and Ike then seem to be debating three questions at once. First, is the pattern of history cyclic or linear? Second, has ownership supplanted the original "holding" of the earth in communal anonymity? Finally, how can whites amortize the debts they owe for their injustice to blacks?

The first question can be answered only by the whole of the narrative. So far both the line and the circle have fit parts of the action, but neither pattern clearly subsumes the other.

The second question is linked to the first. If the pattern is cyclic, then the primal holding might once again be the only legitimate form of possession. If, on the contrary, the pattern is linear, then holding may have given way irrevocably to the other modes of possession. Since the second question depends on the first, it can't be answered yet either; but the text is now rich enough to support an analysis of possession. From its first pages *Go Down, Moses* has dealt with ownership—the McCaslins' holding slaves, controlling tenants, and owning land. "The Old People" raised the issue in a new setting, the wilderness rather than the farm; and the first three parts of "The Bear" developed those rituals and meanings in detail. By fleshing out the history of the McCaslin farm, Part 4 permits at long last a full analysis of the rituals and motifs of possession. The analysis reveals a surprisingly logical form. It carries the original holding through four transformations: owning, taming, sharing, and relinquishing.

Go Down, Moses begins its study of possession in the beginning, in the mythic time when God made the earth and assigned to all people the duty of holding it. Even after the Fall, man's duty remained "to hold the earth mutual and intact in the communal anonymity of brother-

hood, and all the fee [God] asked was pity and humility
and sufferance and endurance and the sweat of his face for
bread" (257). But, according to _Go Down, Moses,_ men fell
again when some of them refused to hold the land but
claimed to own it. The act of claiming ownership cast mankind out of myth and into history, and with this act the
history of the McCaslin land begins. Issetibbeha's fathers
shattered their tribe's communal anonymity by claiming to
own the wilderness where the Indians lived, and Ikkemotubbe repeated the act of dispossession. The act of
seizing the wilderness split the tribe into two groups,
owners and nonowners. As nonowners the Indians were
dispossessed not of land they had owned but of land they
had held. The ritual pattern of transition from holding to
either owning or not owning has occurred over and over
in history, which is a chronicle of dispossession. Sometimes the dispossessed become subjects of the owners of
the land, as the Indians do. At other times, however, the
dispossessed become possessions themselves. Like the
blacks from Africa they become slaves. Yet a third kind of
nonowning exists in addition to being dispossessed and
being possessed. One can continue to hold. Sam Fathers
fits two of the categories. So far as he was black, he was
enslaved; so far as he was an Indian, he continued to hold
the land after Ikkemotubbe had disqualified himself. After
the tribe had been driven west, Sam held the land jointly
with Jobaker, became the only holder on Jobaker's death,
and passed his responsibility for holding the land on to
Ike. At this level the pattern of possession takes the following shape:

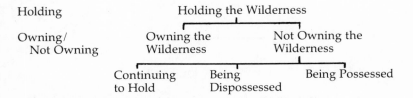

Holding   Holding the Wilderness

Owning/   Owning the   Not Owning the
   Not Owning   Wilderness   Wilderness

          Continuing   Being   Being Possessed
          to Hold   Dispossessed

Within the level of ownership, societies have devised their rituals for transferring possession. Rituals define the acts of buying and selling so that Ikkemotubbe could give a deed to Carothers for "white man's money" and another deed to Sutpen for "money or rum or whatever it was" (254–55). Rituals determine the procedures for bequeathing and inheriting so that the legitimate takes precedence over the illegitimate, the third generation over the fourth, the white over the black, the male over the female, and so on. Thus Carothers' property passes to his twin sons Buck and Buddy and then to Ike as Buck's son. "Was" employs the ritual for dowries; "Pantaloon in Black" touches on the ritual for renting; and the first three stories of the book all use the ritual for winning and losing possessions by wagering. *Go Down, Moses*, however, pushes its treatment of possession far beyond this point.

The taming of some of the wilderness is the next level of the analysis and divides owning into two forms: owning the wilderness and owning the tamed land. Thomas Sutpen had bought a hundred square miles of the wilderness from Ikkemotubbe; and after Sutpen failed to tame it, it was sold to Major de Spain, who, believing he owned it, let it remain wild, a part of the Big Woods that Sam Fathers continued to hold. Carothers likewise had bought land from Ikkemotubbe but had succeeded in taming it, in turning it into the family's farm. As men move from owning to taming, the pattern of possession looks like this:

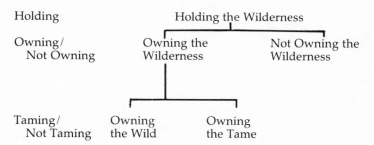

A factual analysis of the ownership of land in the United States might well stop here. The simple pattern of land either wild or tame but inevitably owned would certainly describe most real estate. But that analysis will not do justice to *Go Down, Moses*. Its rituals and motifs of possession go beyond holding, owning, and taming to two more levels: sharing and relinquishing. By using those two levels, the text distinguishes between meanings that usage often blurs. To share is to retain ownership while letting someone else control the use of property. To relinquish is to give up ownership without any legal obligation to do so.

Society is of course familiar with acts of sharing and relinquishing and provides rituals by which to carry out the acts. While still a child, Ike regarded the ledgers as a chronicle of sharing, a record "of all his people, not only the whites but the black one too . . . and of the land which they had all held and used in common and fed from and on and would continue to use in common without regard to color or titular ownership" (268). Seeing the Bear killed, reading the ledgers, and relinquishing the farm do not negate Ike's faith in sharing. His voice and the third-person narrator's join in describing Ike's marriage as the metaphorical settling and sharing of a new world:

> it was the new country, his heritage too as it was the heritage of all, out of the earth, beyond the earth yet of the earth because his too was of the earth's long chronicle, his too because each must share with another in order to come into it and in the sharing they become one: for that while, one: for that little while at least, one. (311)

Even though society has provided rituals for sharing and relinquishing, it regards them as anomalies in the patterns of possession. Neither sharing nor relinquishing has a clear-cut meaning; neither has a motif. Like any new act they might be seen in a variety of ways: as a beneficial reform, as a threat to the established order, as an individual peculiarity, or whatever. The acts await an assignment of meaning. Cass does not understand what Ike means by the act of relinquishment, nor does Ike, who says to him:

I'm trying to explain to the head of my family something
which I have got to do which I dont quite understand myself,
not in justification of it but to explain it if I can. (288)

Since society has no motifs for sharing and relinquishing, readers must search, as Cass and Ike do, for
definitions and examples in the chronicle of the farm.
From the beginning the McCaslins have habitually violated their society's rituals and motifs of possession by
sharing and by relinquishing property. To say that Roth
shares with George in "The Fire and the Hearth" and
Mannie and Rider in "Pantaloon in Black" by renting them
land would probably stretch the point. But other acts
wouldn't. When Lucas married, Cass "built a house for
them and allotted Lucas a specific acreage to be farmed as
he saw fit as long as he lived or remained on the place"
(110). Zack honored that agreement as long as he lived
and insured in his will that Lucas's wife, Molly, would be
cared for as long as she lived, no matter what happened to
Lucas. Despite Lucas's provocations Roth lives up to and
even reconfirms both of these obligations to share possessions.

The McCaslins also relinquish property. Even Carothers
relinquishes by proxy: his will leaves ten acres of land to
Thucydus, who is Roskus's and Fibby's son, and a
thousand dollars to Turl, who is his own son. Buck and
Buddy honor these bequests. When Thucydus declines
the land and the money they offer him instead and says he
wants to work his freedom out, they allow him to do so.
They triple the legacy that Turl never claimed. Again, descendants carry out the relinquishments. Ike tries to find
James to give him his legacy and goes to Arkansas to give
Fonsiba hers. He turns over to Lucas not only Lucas's own
thousand dollars but James's as well.

The addition of these two levels, sharing and relinquishing, completes the diagram of possession and gives it the
following form:

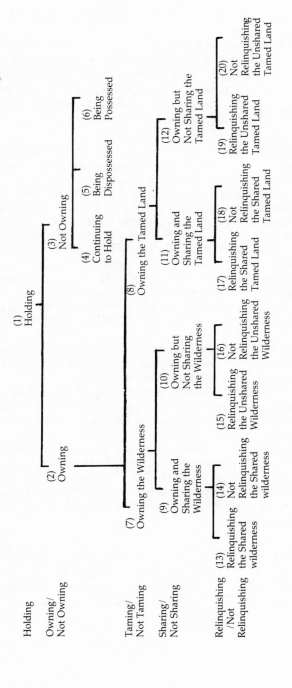

Holding

Owning/
Not Owning

Taming/
Not Taming

Sharing/
Not Sharing

Relinquishing
/Not
Relinquishing

The text provides examples of every category of possession, as will be shown by a brief look at the last level,
categories 13 through 20. The Big Woods is of course the
wilderness, and the farm is the tamed land. The following
analysis, as might be expected, treats money as inter-
changeable with land.

13. *Relinquishing the Shared Wilderness.* De Spain has shared with
    hunters, servants, huntsmen, and even townspeople the
    Big Woods he owns. After the Bear's death de Spain relin-
    quishes the burial plot and returns it to the wilderness.
14. *Not Relinquishing the Shared Wilderness.* De Spain sells the rest
    of his land in the Big Woods to the lumber company.
15. *Relinquishing the Unshared Wilderness.* After inheriting the Big
    Woods, Sutpen's heirs temporarily relinquished it by letting
    it go wild.
16. *Not Relinquishing the Unshared Wilderness.* Neither Ik-
    kemotubbe nor Sutpen ever relinquished land. Sutpen
    meant to tame his and establish a great plantation. His heirs
    in the end did not relinquish it either but sold it to de Spain
    (191).
17. *Relinquishing the Shared Tamed Land.* Ike relinquishes to Cass
    the ownership of the farm, the land that blacks and whites
    "had all held and used in common" (268).
18. *Not Relinquishing the Shared Tamed Land.* McCaslins bequeath
    and inherit the farm; and although Ike relinquishes it, Cass
    does not. He bequeaths it all to Zack, even the land turned
    over to Lucas; and Zack leaves it all to Roth.
19. *Relinquishing the Unshared Tamed Land.* Carothers relin-
    quished land to Thucydus and left Turl money.
20. *Not Relinquishing the Unshared Tamed Land.* Hubert
    Beauchamp's farm and all other unshared property handed
    down in accordance with society's rules for possession fits
    this category.

   The diagram as it stands appears to suggest that alterna-
tives are equally viable. They are not, and the fact that
they are not affects the meaning of sharing and relinquishing in *Go Down, Moses.* To see such meanings, we must

consider what happens to property that passes through the levels.

Ownership dooms the wilderness, whether shared or unshared, except for whatever can be relinquished but still protected, set aside like the burial plot. When Sutpen's heirs let his land revert to the wild, they empty category 16 into 15. Category 15 then empties into 9 when they sell the land to de Spain, who shares it for a time. After the Bear's death de Spain sells most of the land to the lumber company, which will destroy the wilderness, thereby leaving category 14 empty. In category 13, however, the burial plot remains. Of all the wilderness only that category, land shared and then relinquished, endures.

As the Big Woods stands for the wilderness, so Carothers McCaslin's and Hubert Beauchamp's farms are the archetypes of the tamed land. Since neither man shares land while he lives, their farms remain in category 12. Two weeks after Ike's birth Hubert announces his intention to relinquish property to Ike, who is his godson. Hubert wraps in burlap a silver goblet filled with gold pieces as a gift for Ike to open on his twenty-first birthday. When Ike is six, Hubert falls on bad times; and the "burlap lump" changes its shape overnight (306). On opening the gift when he is twenty-one, Ike finds not the goblet but a tin coffeepot filled with Hubert's IOU's. Thus the unshared and unrelinquished property in category 20 is consumed and destroyed. The property in 19, unshared but finally relinquished, has lost its worth and become the coffeepot and the "rat's nest" of IOU's. Property that is shared, on the other hand, is neither consumed nor turned into trash. After Carothers dies, his farm moves from category 12 to 11 by being shared in accordance with his will and with the beliefs that Buck and Buddy put into practice. On Hubert's death his land too passes from the unshared category to the shared by passing into the McCaslins' hands. Often, as we have seen, the McCaslins relinquish property. Ike carries out the greatest act of relinquishment in handing the farm to Cass. Yet Ike's relinquishment merely transfers the land to Cass, who continues to share it but wills to his own descendants the title to the land. Category 17 thus turns ineluctably into 18: what Ike relinquished, Cass and his heirs never relinquish but continue to share.

These processes leave only two viable states of possession, categories 13 and 18. The wilderness survives if relinquished; otherwise it is destroyed. The tamed land endures if it is owned but shared; otherwise it is consumed or reduced to worthlessness. The outcome of the processes sheds light on the question of whether owning has irrevocably supplanted holding. The answer is, as one might by now expect, a paradoxical no-and-yes. In the eyes of the law de Spain still owns the last piece of wilderness, the burial plot. The Edmondses still own the farm. Ownership has not been abolished. Yet the harshness of the original acts of dispossession has been mitigated by acts of sharing and relinquishing. Slowly, very slowly, owners—both the McCaslins and the Edmondses—have begun to think of themselves as holders and have started sharing their property with nonowners, with Thucydus, Turl, James, Sophonsiba, Lucas, and Molly. At the very start of the whole narrative, in the opening of "Was," Ike is described as "merely holding" the bungalow his wife had left him, holding it for "his wife's sister and her children who had lived in it with him since his wife's death" (4). To share thus becomes a way of holding, and the line from holding through owning and taming to sharing and relinquishing may circle back toward the start. While men can never return to the mythic time when they held the earth mutual and intact in the communal anonymity of brotherhood, they may find out through sharing and relinquishing how to live together. On the McCaslin land, in particular, people may be advancing toward an historical way of holding the land.

Is history then flowing away from ownership and toward holding? Cass and Ike, despite their differences,

agree that it is. Both men see in their family's history signs
that the McCaslins are carrying out, however slowly,
God's will by establishing on the farm and in the wilderness—that is, in history—the life God intended for the
New World, a life "founded in humility and pity and sufferance and pride of one to another" (258).

At this point in their discussion Cass and Ike begin to
work out their replies to the third question: how can
whites amortize the debts they owe for their injustice toward blacks? Both men accept one basic answer—by
mitigating the evils of possession—and they consider
three means for mitigation: sharing, relinquishing, and
suffering. Both men agree that, despite the injustices that
the McCaslins have committed, their family has had an
unusual tradition of sharing and relinquishing. The
ledgers' record of the transformation of slaves from
property into people and then into members of the family
supports Cass and Ike in that belief. The narrative presents its twenty-page summary of the ledgers in the middle of the discussion of the pattern of history since the
creation. Yet the summary is no interruption; instead, it
makes explicit the family history that both men know by
heart, the history against which they test their ideas about
God's will for the world. Since "The Bear" is the story of
how Ike came to relinquish the farm, the narrative treats
the summary from his viewpoint; and as the summary
begins, Ike imagines that God Himself also finds in the
ledgers the pattern of history that runs from dispossession
toward holding:

> To him it was as though the ledgers in their scarred cracked
> leather bindings were being lifted down one by one in their
> fading sequence and spread open on the desk or perhaps
> upon some apocryphal Bench or even Altar or perhaps before
> the Throne Itself for a last perusal and contemplation and
> refreshment of the Allknowledgeable before the yellowed
> pages and the brown thin ink in which was recorded the
> injustice and a little at least of its amelioration and restitution

faded back forever into the anonymous communal original dust. (261)

The pattern of amelioration and restitution in the family's history thus confirms the broader patterns that Cass and Ike believe they have discovered in history and in God's will.

The summary began, as I said, in the middle of their discussion. Ike and Cass took stands that seem opposed. Ike contended that no one can own land; Cass replied that men do nevertheless own it. Ike countered with an interpretation of history and the Bible. By claiming the land, he said, men had dispossessed both their fellow men and God and had thereby tainted and cursed the land. God had chosen Carothers as the "seed progenitive of the three generations" of McCaslins who would accomplish at least a little of God's aim "to set at least some of His lowly people free" (259). Cass challenged Ike to explain how he had verified his interpretation since history shows such slim progress toward that end and since the Bible often contradicts itself. "The heart already knows," Ike replied (260). Although the response seems weak, Cass accepted it. For him, as for Ike, there is no other way to account for their family's history. "And perhaps you are right," Cass said and went on to discover for himself in history not only Buck and Buddy carrying out God's aim but a "thousand other Bucks and Buddies in less than two generations" (261). At that point the narrative summarizes the ledgers and then picks up this discussion exactly where it broke off. But now readers share Cass's and Ike's knowledge—and their guilt. In learning the ledgers' story, the family's history, we have also come to see that the McCaslins' story is intertwined with ours—with the history of the South, the nation, the New World, Western culture, and all creation. We must consequently recognize that Cass and Ike are not debating the meaning merely of their acts but of ours. Their discussion calls into question all of our societies' rituals and motifs of possession.

Now Cass and Ike no longer seem to oppose each other. While they are not in accord and never will be, they are now cooperating in working out the implications of their history and their beliefs. Cass's first statement internalizes the conflict between the positions he and Ike seemed to take earlier:

> More men than that one Buck and Buddy to fumble-heed that truth so mazed for them that spoke it and so confused for them that heard yet still there was 1865. (282)

He accepts as "truth" Ike's interpretation of the Bible and his view of history as taking shape around the efforts of people like Buck and Buddy to grasp that truth and embody it in their acts. But why then, he wonders, did men have to fight the Civil War? Just as Cass's new position has moved toward Ike's, so Ike's explanation shares some of Cass's original skepticism and realism. Although there were more men than Buck and Buddy, Ike says, there were not enough. God grew disappointed:

> at last He saw that they were all Grandfather all of them and that even from them the elected and chosen the best the very best He could expect (not hope mind: not hope) would be Bucks and Buddies and not even enough of them and in the third generation not even Bucks and Buddies but . . . an Isaac . . . repudiating immolation: fatherless and therefore safe declining the altar because maybe this time the exasperated Hand might not supply the kid. (283)

The pessimism that Cass has abandoned Ike has picked up. According to Ike, men's deeds in the New World that God had meant for "a refuge and sanctuary of liberty and freedom" made even God declare, *"This will do. This is enough"* (283). But before God could call down the Apocalypse, John Brown said, *"I am just against the weak because they are niggers being held in bondage by the strong just because they are white"* (285), took down his gun, and so saved the world from destruction. Ike's view of John

Brown as a hero would certainly offend Southerners, who
have traditionally regarded him as a bloodthirsty fanatic
and a madman; and when Ike immediately adds that, because of Brown, God "turned once more to this land
which He still intended to save," Cass is astonished at the
notion of the Civil War as a boon. "Turned back to us?" he
says. "His face to us?" (285).

Yet, as Ike explains his view, Cass again finds that he in
large measure shares it. Before the Civil War, Ike says,
God looked down on the South, which held slaves, and
the North, which grew fat on the profits of slavery; and He
saw that the New World was as corrupt as the Old. Of
course, there were exceptions. Bucks and Buddies tried to
learn to be just:

> wives and daughters at least made soups and jellies for
> [slaves] when they were sick and carried the trays through
> the mud and the winter too into the stinking cabins and sat in
> the stinking cabins and kept fires going until crises came and
> passed but that was not enough: and when they were very
> sick had them carried into the big house itself into the com-
> pany room itself maybe and nursed them there which the
> white man would have done too for any other of his cattle
> that was sick but at least the man who hired one from a livery
> wouldn't have and still that was not enough. (285)

John Brown's gun, however, suggested to God another
way by which men might redeem themselves, and so He
said to Himself, *"Apparently they can learn nothing save
through suffering, remember nothing save when underlined in
blood"* (286). Cass, not yet convinced, cites the misfortunes
that afflicted the Confederate army—Lee's battle order
dropped on a saloon floor and discovered by a Yankee
intelligence officer; Jackson and then Longstreet shot in
the night by their own patrols—and accuses the Southern
leaders of personal foolhardiness that hurt their cause.
"His face to us?" he says again (286). Ike, more traditionally Southern here, asks:

Who else could have made [the Yankees] fight: could have
struck them so aghast with fear and dread as to turn shoulder
to shoulder and face one way and even stop talking for a
while . . . except Jackson in the Valley and three separate
armies trying to catch him and none of them ever knowing
whether they were just retreating from a battle or just running into one and Stuart riding his whole command entirely
around the biggest single armed force this continent ever saw
in order to see what it looked like from behind. (288)

Cass comes to agree on the whole that suffering has been
redemptive. "Well, maybe that's what He wanted. At
least, that's what He got," not only from the war but also
from Reconstruction, which the two men see as "that dark
corrupt and bloody time while three separate peoples"—
the blacks, the Southern whites, and the Northerners—
"had tried to adjust not only to one another but to the new
land which they had created and inherited too and must
live in for the reason that those who had lost it were no
less free to quit it than those who had gained it were"
(289).

Here then the line of history and beliefs, of acts and
meanings, running back from the present moment in the
commissary to the Creation deepens the significance of
the family history inscribed in the ledgers. That history
points toward the future, toward sharing the tamed land,
toward a sharing that will help white men amortize their
debts to blacks and that, while it can never abolish
ownership and restore holding, can ameliorate the evil of
ownership, of being dispossessed and of being possessed.

The ledgers themselves likewise point toward the future.

McCaslin lifted them down daily now to write into them the
continuation of that record which two hundred years had not
been enough to complete and another hundred would not be
enough to discharge; that chronicle which was a whole land
in miniature, which multiplied and compounded was the en-

tire South, twenty-three years after surrender and twenty-four from emancipation. (293)

On the pages of the ledgers one column records the supplies provided to those who farm the land; the other column records the value of the cotton they grew. The two columns form the "threads frail as truth and impalpable as equators yet cable-strong to bind for life them who made the cotton to the land their sweat fell on" (293–94).

In those words the third-person narrator defines the limit beyond which Cass cannot go in accepting the way Ike is explaining, to himself as well as to Cass, why he has repudiated his heritage and relinquished the land. The men have agreed on many points: on the illegitimacy of the transition from holding to owning, on the desirability of restoring some sort of holding, on the white man's need to repay blacks for his injustices, and on the view that farming, the actual dropping of sweat onto soil, has bound blacks to the land. Here, though, Ike and Cass come to a parting of the ways as they face this question: given all that they have agreed on—God's will, the shape of mankind's history, and the nature of their family's heritage—what should they do now? The last twenty pages of Part 4 present their opposing opinions, not so much in articulated argument as in memories, gestures, and images juxtaposed against one another.

According to Ike, the two threads, the cost of supplies and the profits from crops, do not bind him; and so he can relinquish the farm. The threads do of course bind blacks to the land and will continue to do so for several generations, a period he thinks of as "a little while." With nary a qualm about how blacks themselves might view the prospect of years of bondage, Ike regards the time as short. It seems so to him because he is certain that blacks will "endure," whatever that means. In explaining himself, Ike reveals most clearly his penchant for opposition, for the pattern X/Y. "They will outlast us," he says, "because they are . . . better than we are. Stronger than we are.

Their vices are vices aped from white men or that white men and bondage have taught them: improvidence and intemperance and evasion—not laziness: evasion. . . ." Cass listens skeptically, adds a few more vices, and concludes the list with "inability to distinguish between mine and thine." Ike counters that one devastatingly: "How distinguish, when for two hundred years mine did not even exist for them?" (294), and Cass tells him to go on and list the virtues. Blacks' vices are our vices, Ike says, but their virtues are their own, endurance ("So have mules," Cass says), but Ike goes on: ". . . and pity and tolerance and forbearance and fidelity and love of children . . ." ("So have dogs," says Cass). In another context the analogies to animals would surely be denigrating. Here though they don't have quite that effect because in *Go Down, Moses* and "The Bear" and even the discussion itself animals do not stand lower than men. Indeed, Sam and Ike look up to totem animals like the deer and the Bear, and Boon serves Lion. Through animals men can return to their roots, a point that Ike immediately makes by saying that blacks did not learn their virtues from whites but inherited them "from the old free fathers a longer time free than us because we have never been free" (295). Ike himself has been, as both men recall, the pupil of the Bear and the fyce. From their lessons he has acquired virtues and learned that the only lasting way to possess the wilderness that they once shared is to relinquish it. Once relinquished, the wilderness can be shared in this life as the burial plot is shared and can be shared in the next world through the life-in-death. Ike has reached the state in which he will "never need to grieve" over the wilderness, as the young man in Keats's ode never needs to grieve over the girl, *"because he could never approach any nearer and would never have to get any further away"* (297). Ike means to apply the same principle to the tamed land. By relinquishing the farm, he hopes to free himself from his heritage, from his responsibility to amortize the injustices of the past. He hopes to sever X and Y.

But Cass's "bitter smiling" shows how far he and Ike are apart, "the two of them juxtaposed and alien now to each other against their ravaged patrimony"—the farm ravaged by the evils that flow from possession and the wilderness where both men were initiated, the Big Woods now ravaged by the lumber company. Cass comprehends Ike's stand but refuses to make it his own. His voice and that of the text itself undertake to criticize Ike's view. "Habet then," Cass says, the Latin for "he owns" denoting individual ownership as opposed to communal holding and connoting the legal language of deeds and the antiquity of possession. "So this land is, indubitably, of and by itself cursed," Cass goes on (297–98). By repeating the word *cursed*, Cass alludes skeptically to Ike's view, expressed forty pages earlier, that "maybe it was more than justice that only the white man's blood was available and capable to raise the white man's curse" (259). The text supports Cass's skepticism and deepens it into irony for the reader who recalls Ike's meeting with Fonsiba and her husband in Arkansas. It was winter, and they were living in a log cabin in a "pathless waste of unfenced fallow and wilderness jungle" (277). The husband had not built a barn or cut enough wood to last the night or penned in their last hog. He was counting on government pension checks to suffice for their support. Ike finds him dressed like a minister and sitting in the cabin's only chair reading a book through spectacles without lenses. There in a "desolation" (278) that is neither wilderness nor farm, Ike proclaims his doctrine:

> "Dont you see? This whole land, the whole South, is cursed, and all of us who derive from it, whom it ever suckled, white and black both, lie under the curse? Granted that my people brought the curse onto the land: maybe for that reason their descendants alone can—not resist it, not combat it—maybe just endure and outlast it until the curse is lifted. Then your peoples' turn will come because we have forfeited ours. But not now. Not yet. Dont you see?" (278)

Removing his "lenseless spectacles" and holding them in a "workless" hand, the husband concurs. He sees that the white man's rituals of ownership have cursed the land and goes on to assert in the vacuous tones of political rhetoric that the Civil War and Emancipation have brought the millennium.

"The curse you whites brought into this land has been lifted. It has been voided and discharged. We are seeing a new era, an era dedicated, as our founders intended it, to freedom, liberty and equality for all, to which this country will be the new Canaan." (279)

The husband is waiting for the milk and honey to flow. Ike and the third-person narrator object. The narrator calls the husband's notion the "imbecility of the boundless folly and the baseless hope," and even Ike knows that the land, cursed or not, will require work from those who live on it. He dismisses the husband as "foolish." Nevertheless, both men share the notion of the curse.

It is with pity, on the contrary, that Ike looks on Fonsiba, who crouches behind a table in a corner. She watches him "without alarm" yet "without recognition" because, by marrying, she has cut herself off from the South and the McCaslin family. For that separation she has had to pay a high price: in the midst of that desolation and with a fool of a husband she watches Ike "without hope." "Fonsiba," he says, "Fonsiba. Are you all right?" She answers simply, "I'm free" (280). She has willingly paid the price, but one may doubt that she can ever be free of the past.

For the reader, then, Cass's use of the word *cursed* calls up comparisons between Ike and Fonsiba's husband, especially when Ike confirms it by repeating it. In his meeting with the husband Ike had

jerked his arm, comprehensive, almost violent: whereupon it all seemed to stand there about them . . . the empty fields without plow or seed to work them, fenceless against the

stock which did not exist within or without the walled stable
which likewise was not there. (279)

Cass too raises his hand but calls up a vision of quite
another landscape, a vision condensing the family's heritage, the history of the farm, and its future.

> as the stereopticon condenses into one instantaneous field the
> myriad minutia [sic] of its scope, so did that slight and rapid
> gesture establish in the small cramped and cluttered twilit
> room not only the ledgers but the whole plantation in its
> mazed and intricate entirety. (298)

This land is not desolate: it threatens no one with starva-
tion. Its fields feed and clothe and even "pay a little cash
money at Christmas-time" to the people who work it. Cass
objects to Ike's view because Cass has different bases for
his beliefs. While juxtaposition is typical of Ike, Cass tends
toward condensation, toward the complex union of apparently disparate elements, toward $X = Y$. Consequently, in
his vision the farm, like the South and the nation and the
New World and all, is no Canaan but an "edifice intricate
and complex and founded upon injustice and erected by
ruthless rapacity and carried on even yet with at times
downright savagery not only to the human beings but the
valuable animals too, yet solvent and efficient and, more
than that: not only still intact but enlarged, increased . . ."
(298). Under Cass's hand the farm had survived the war
and Reconstruction and, according to the vision, will continue "intact and still increasing." He knows that there can
never again be equality for all and that men will never be
able to return to the Eden of the communal anonymity of
brotherhood. Yet although men will never inhabit a land
of milk and honey, Cass foresees the growth of the farm,
the spread of sharing so long as Cass and "his McCaslin
successors" last—that is, so long as the family's heritage of
sharing endures "even though their surnames might not
even be Edmonds then" (298). Thus, while Ike chooses
relinquishment, Cass chooses sharing.

The narrative turns next to the third means of mitigation: suffering. Ike reacts sharply to the name *McCaslin* because it emphasizes what pains Ike most, the guilt he suffers for his family's sins, particularly those of Carothers. "Habet too," Ike says. "Because that's it: not the land, but us" (298). Carothers, he goes on, owns not just the land but all his descendants.

> "Not only the blood, but the name too; not only its color but its designation: Edmonds, white, but, a female line, could have no other but the name his father bore; Beauchamp, the elder line and the male one, but, black, could have had any name he liked and no man would have cared, except the name his father bore who had no name." (298–99)

Here Cass interrupts because Ike has left out the primary blood and name, "the male, the eldest, the direct and sole and white and still McCaslin even, father to son to son," the line that fits the rituals of possession, the lineage of Ike himself. The omission is a sign of Ike's dominant aim: he hopes to avoid suffering by cutting the ties that bind him to his family and its sins. Therefore, at that moment, he relinquishes the land and repudiates his heritage. He declares, "I am free" (299).

That declaration juxtaposes Ike's stand to Fonsiba's and especially Cass's. Ike's words echo hers. Although never a slave, she was truly one of the dispossessed and, giving up the security of the farm her relatives owned, had knowingly chosen freedom, even if freedom entailed suffering. Her "I'm free" expressed her pathetic desire to heal the wounds that history and the McCaslin family, her family, had inflicted on her. Even so, she could not do so entirely. Ike followed her and set up the trust fund on which she and her husband might someday have to depend for their very food. In Ike's mouth, too, the words are pathetic. They express the agony of guilt he suffers that drives him to relinquish the farm. Still, one feels less sympathy for Ike than for Fonsiba. As a black and a

woman she is not guilty of injustices, but Ike has inherited
a heavy responsibility as a white McCaslin man.

Ike's stand and Cass's also oppose one another. On
hearing Ike proclaim himself free, Cass needs to make no
gesture toward the family's history or the farm, "no infer-
ence of fading pages, no postulation of the stereoptic
whole" (299), because both men perceive their heritage as
linking them to the past. Ike, following the pattern X/Y,
dreams of severing the link. He hopes that relinquishment
will cut him free from responsibility and therefore from
suffering. Cass, following the pattern X = Y, has no such
dreams. He doubts that anyone can escape from the past
and from responsibility. He wonders whether Ike's view
can even account for Ike's own experience and beliefs.
Although Cass has conceded that God chose the McCaslins to carry out His aims, any successes He will achieve
through Ike will take a long time coming:

> it took Him a bear and an old man and four years just for you.
> And it took you fourteen years to reach that point and about
> that many, maybe more, for Old Ben, and more than seventy
> for Sam Fathers. And you are just one. How long then? How
> long? (299)

"It will be long," Ike admits. "I have never said otherwise." But he repeats his assurance that "it will be all right
because they will endure." Cass recoils from that prospect
and says, "And anyway, you will be free." His words are
bitter and maybe even contemptuous. To him Ike seems to
be trying, and futilely at that, to evade responsibility by
clinging to his heritage from Sam while casting off his
family heritage. Cass denies the possibility of such freedom. "No," he cries, "not now nor ever, we from them
nor they from us." Blacks and whites, he says, are so
bound together by the past that no emancipation, no relinquishment, can ever free either one from the other. Cass
therefore rejects Ike's view: "So I repudiate too. I would
deny even if I knew it were true. I would have to. Even

you can see that I could do no else. I am what I am; I will be always what I was born and have always been" (299—300).

With those words Cass defines his own stand. While Ike chooses to relinquish, Cass chooses to share. The burdens that Ike wants to throw off, Cass willingly shoulders. He accepts the burden that Ike can escape, the responsibility for preserving the farm and all who depend on it, and the burden that Ike naively hopes to evade, the responsibility for the past and the necessity to suffer in order to mitigate the injustices of history. Cass declares that he is not alone in taking his stand. "More than me," he says, "just as there were more than Buck and Buddy in what you called His first plan which failed." But when Ike says, "And more than me," thereby claiming to belong to that lineage, Cass rejects his claim: "No. Not even you." Instead, Cass defines the heritage that Ike is truly claiming, the heritage of Sam Fathers:

> "You said how on that instant when Ikkemotubbe realised that he could sell the land to Grandfather, it ceased forever to have been his. All right; go on: Then it belonged to Sam Fathers, old Ikkemotubbe's son. And who inherited from Sam Fathers, if not you?" (300)

Ike's "Yes" accepts that lineage; and by saying "Sam Fathers set me free," he declares his allegiance to the wilderness. His act accords with what he learned as Sam's pupil. In the wilderness the act most like holding is relinquishing, as the burial plot is relinquished. But in the tamed land if one owner relinquishes property, it simply passes to a new owner. There relinquishment is no more than a futile gesture, while sharing actually ameliorates the condition of the dispossessed. Cass, who pays his allegiance to the tamed land, therefore accepts the farm and shares it with blacks. Cass chooses to remain on the farm and embroiled in society. Ike, however, yearning to escape from the farm and the entanglements of family and society, rejects the farm and undertakes two conflicting occupations. On the one hand, he sets up as a carpenter. The voices of Ike and the third-person narrator join to explain his odd reason for choosing that work: ". . . if the Nazarene had found carpentering good for the life and ends He had assumed and elected to serve, it would be all right too for Isaac McCaslin . . ." (309). Ike thus becomes a carpenter in imitation of Christ. Yet his own aims puzzle him: ". . . Isaac McCaslin's ends, although simple enough in their apparent motivation, were and would be always incomprehensible to him . . ." (309–10). They are puzzling because for Ike, as for the narrative, both $X = Y$ and X/Y are true. Ike knows that he is and is not adhering to Christ's model. Christ bore the burden of man's sins; Ike has rejected it. He has not merely asked God to let the cup pass from him but has shoved it away. Ike does not seek crucifixion or any other form of ritual suicide. Sam, the Bear, and Rider all found ways to die; Ike does not. To choose an occupation because it was Christ's is to take Christ for a model, but only in a trivial way. That reason for becoming a carpenter mocks Ike. His chosen occupation also mocks his initiation under the tutelage of Sam and the Bear. They treasured the Big Woods; he builds with the lumber from its very trees. On the other hand, while Ike earns his living as a carpenter, his true vocation is that of the woodsman, his true setting the wilderness. Whereas Cass chooses to live in the complexities of history and social life, Ike prefers the simplicity of myth and the wilderness. Maybe he wishes to live in harmony with nature and myth as Sam did or to find the life-in-death in which Mannie and the spirit-deer participated and which Rider and Sam sought. What he finds instead is the reverse, a kind of death-in-life. The text itself joins Cass in criticizing Ike by portraying him as immature, sterile, and self-deceived. The narrative throws just such shadows over Ike immediately after he says, "Sam Fathers set me free." The next sentence alludes to the rest of his life as long, childless, cramped, and filled, so far as anything filled it, with possessions—his tools, bought with money from Cass; his hunting gear, received as gifts and bequests; and the coffeepot, his legacy from Hubert. The text also criticizes Ike by placing the history of that legacy just after the relinquishment and by comparing Ike and Hubert. In "The Fire and the Hearth" the narrative described Ike as growing younger until in his seventies he had "acquired something of a young boy's high and selfless innocence" (106). There the description might have been taken as praise; at any rate it did not sound like criticism. But "The Bear" portrays Hubert on his deathbed as "still the boy innocent" (306). Furthermore, Hubert's relinquishment is shown to be futile. Unable to speak, he has the burlap parcel brought to his bed; and with his eyes he attempts to convey some message to Ike while holding out but not releasing the parcel, "the hands still clinging . . . even while relinquishing it" (306). His gifts' value has been consumed. He dies having relinquished nothing. Being compared with Hubert undercuts Ike. Another telling comparison is that between the gold pieces in Hubert's goblet and the banknotes Cass tosses onto Ike's bed the night after the relinquishment. Cass and Ike both think that Hubert had "dreamed" of taking the coins back as "merely a loan: nay, a partnership" (307). Ike tries to accept the banknotes in the same way: "As a loan. From you" (308). But Cass refuses to permit that subterfuge and arranges a fifty-dollar-a-month allowance for Ike as Ike had set up the trust for Fonsiba. He will not let Ike believe that he has cut himself free of the farm.

Ike's marriage also demonstrates the weakness of his position. All the complexities that he had hoped to escape rise up to surround him. Relinquishment has not isolated or even insulated him from societal relationships and from suffering. About his courtship and marriage the narrative tells little beyond a conversation about possession and family relationships. When Ike misleadingly tells his wife-to-be that he and Cass share ownership, she asks, "Was there a will leaving half of it to him?" He misrepresents the situation slightly by saying, "There didn't need to be a will. His grandmother was my father's sister. We were the same as brothers." She straightens that out immediately: "You are the same as second cousins and that's all you ever will be." Her next remark—"But I dont suppose it matters" (311)—is ambiguous. It might mean that possessions don't interest her, but her subsequent acts imply that she means that his relinquishment does not matter because she believes that she can make Ike reclaim the farm as Buck reclaimed the big house after his marriage.

At first Ike and his wife lived in a boarding house. To surprise her, he builds a bungalow; but before it is finished, she hears rumors that she and Ike will move soon. Assuming that the farm will now be theirs, she thinks she has succeeded and gratefully seduces Ike. He scarcely tries to disillusion her until, just before intercourse, she whispers, "Promise." Ike will not renege on his relinquishment and says a bit hysterically, "No. No. No, I tell you. I wont. I cant. Never." Still he feels her hand on him: she has not given up. Again he refuses; but her hand, "steady and invincible," finally draws from him an ambiguous "Yes," not to her desire to possess the farm but to his desire to possess her. At the same time Ike condemns her as a temptress: *She is lost. She was born lost.* Instantly he extends his condemnation to himself. He feels caught between the sterility of relinquishment and the desire to live. His plight seems to him to result from the curse on all possessing. *"We were all born lost,"* he thinks (314). After intercourse his wife knows that he has refused and rages at him: "And that's all. That's all from me. If this dont get you that son you talk about, it wont be mine" (315).

With this guaranteeing of sterility and of the end of the legitimate male line of white McCaslins, Part 4 ends. The earliest passage of the text has told us that the guarantee was kept: Isaac McCaslin remained "father to no one." As a result he never escaped from suffering, as earlier passages also confirm. The futility of his relinquishment shamed him. "The Fire and the Hearth" records his belief that Lucas knows that *"I reneged, cried calf-rope, sold my birthright, betrayed my blood, for what he too calls not peace but obliteration . . ."* (109). Relinquishment did not even buy him obliteration because, as the Bear tried to teach him by leading him back to his watch and compass, he could not immerse himself in the wilderness. As a man he could never exist outside of society, and there he was bound to suffer. Maybe in the life-in-death there is "no heart to be driven and outraged, no flesh to be mauled and bled" (329), but in this life all must suffer.

His act of relinquishment also opposes the sharing that is inherent in marriage where "each must share with another in order to come into" the human heritage "and in the sharing they become one: for that while, one: for that little while at least, one" (311). Again this part of "The Bear" adds to the significance of a passage in "The Fire and the Hearth" that shows the pain that relinquishment has inflicted on both Ike and his wife. She is bitter at never having come to possess the farm; and his feelings conflict with one another: he looks on her "peacefully and with pity for her and regret too, for her, for both of them." Without complaining he lets her make sarcastic remarks about the relinquishment:

> It didn't matter. He could ask her forgiveness as loudly thus as if he had shouted, express his pity and grief; husband and wife did not need to speak words to one another . . . because . . . they had touched and become as God when they voluntarily and in advance forgave one another for all that each knew the other could never be. (107–8)

The conclusion of Part 4 is thus not entirely conclusive. The tragic romance of Parts 1, 2, and 3 has been replaced by the irony of Ike's failed quest for freedom from history, society, and suffering. Two of the questions being debated in Part 4 remain unanswered. We cannot tell whether the pattern of history is linear or cyclic, and we cannot be certain that sharing and relinquishing are equivalent to a restoration of holding. We do know, however, that by sharing the tamed land and relinquishing the wilderness, white men can amortize the debts they have incurred by their injustice to the dispossessed. All in all, Part 4 has favored condensation over juxtaposition, sharing over relinquishing, the linear pattern of history over the cyclic pattern of myth, and therefore Cass's position over Ike's. While Ike's relinquishment has been discredited, the narrative as a whole does not discredit him. Instead, against the weight of Part 4 it has set the weight of the first three parts of "The Bear," "The Old People," and to some extent "Pantaloon in Black," where juxtaposition, the wilderness, relinquishing, and myth are dominant.

Part 5, the final part of "The Bear," remains to be weighed. If Part 4 is set against the earlier sections, how does Part 5 affect the balance of the narrative? Why is it located at the end of "The Bear" instead of appearing after Part 3, where chronology would put it? Looking back to the first three parts of "The Bear" provides a clue. They presented the acts and meaning of the hunt in the wilderness. Part 4 was grounded in the relinquishment scene but glanced back to Ike's reading the ledgers and ahead to his marriage. By treating these scenes out of chronological order, the narrative clustered within Part 4 the acts and motifs related to the farm. Part 4 showed how Ike's initiation and the Bear's death contributed to Ike's decision to relinquish the farm and thus how acts in the wilderness affected the tamed land. Part 5 then moves back to the wilderness and clusters subsequent acts there to reveal how Ike's initiation and the Bear's death also affected the wilderness itself. Clustering thus juxtaposes scene against scene, the wilderness in the first three parts against the farm in the fourth and the farm there against the wilderness again in the fifth.

That juxtaposition, however, isn't enough to account for the placement of Part 5. In fact, a neater contrast would have resulted from combining the last part with the first three and juxtaposing all four wilderness sections against the single farm section in a clearcut X/Y pattern of static juxtaposition. As the fabula shows, such an arrangement would also place the parts more nearly in chronological order and thus in the linear, historical pattern (. . . X → Y → Z . . .) of dynamic juxtaposition. By placing Part 5 at the end, the narrative resists resolution.

Its resistance goes deeper than merely arranging its scenes as wilderness/farm/wilderness instead of wilderness/farm and violating chronology by putting Z between X and Y. There are other ways by which Part 5 also maintains—in fact, cultivates—inconclusiveness. It employs both of the patterns of action, the dynamic patterns of history and myth. Through Ike's eyes it recounts how de Spain disposed of the Big Woods and conveys Ike's perception of the preservation of the wilderness in the mythic cycles of nature and of the life-in-death in which Sam, Lion, and the Bear, each beyond suffering, continue "the long chase" (329). Part 5 also employs both of the static patterns of meaning, those of juxtaposition and condensation. It places Ike in society (with de Spain) and out of it (alone on the train), in again with Ash and out again while Ike walks to the gum tree, and finally in society when he meets Boon at the tree. The text juxtaposes the planing-mill and the wilderness. Ike looks at the mill with "shocked and grieved amazement" and then, hoping not to "look any more," turns to escape from society into the wilderness "within which he would be able to hide himself from it once more anyway" (318). Through metonymy the text related the mill and the train and then through simile equates the train, as it enters the woods, with a "small dingy harmless snake vanishing into weeds" (318). Two implications of the simile appear to conflict with Ike's feelings. Can he regard the train as harmless and the woods as weeds? The train had been harmless once, Ike thinks, as he remembers the story of how Boon and Ash had protected a half-grown bear that the train had treed. They had sat beneath the sapling to keep hunters from shooting the little bear. The train had seemed harmless even a year or two ago when Ike hunted deer that leaped across the tracks from wilderness to wilderness. But the train is harmless no longer; it has doomed the wilderness. Here the narrative takes a surprising tack. A metonymy makes Ike and the train equivalent.

> this time it was as though the train (and not only the train but himself, not only his vision which had seen it and his memory which remembered it but his clothes too, as garments carry back into the clean edgeless blowing of air the lingering effluvium of a sickroom or of death) had brought with it into the doomed wilderness even before the actual axe the shadow and portent of the new mill. (321)

The metonymy, like the Bear, emphasizes that Ike is not at one with the wilderness but carries, despite himself, the effluvium of history, society, and the tamed land. On the train Ike was alone but was not in the wilderness. Getting off the train, he enters the wilderness but is no longer alone because Ash has come to meet him. The snake is transformed from metaphor into threat. Ash warns, ". . . watch your feet. They're crawling" (323). Once Ash leaves, Ike finds himself "in the woods, not alone but solitary," and perceives the mythic cycle of the earth. As that cycle manifests itself, he forgets what is actually happening to the woods and thinks, "They did not change, and, timeless, would not, anymore than would the green of summer and the fire and rain of fall and the iron cold and sometimes even snow . . ." (323). That vision of "timeless" unity is interrupted by his memory of the quietly comic hunting expedition on which Ash had tried to shoot a yearling bear. Once that memory ends, the vision continues: ". . . summer, and fall, and snow, and wet and saprife spring in their ordered immortal sequence." Metaphors condense opposing family relationships in the next phrases. The wilderness is Ike's mother and was "mother and father both" to Sam, who had been Ike's "spirit's father if any had." The maternal wilderness will also be, even if Ike marries, "his mistress and his wife" (326). Their relationship will be incestuous, paradoxical.

Ike finds the burial plot on the knoll. Concrete markers fix the boundaries of the plot that de Spain had reserved out of the woods he sold. Although protecting the plot of wilderness, the markers stand juxtaposed to their setting, "lifeless and shockingly alien in that place where dissolution itself was a seething turmoil of ejaculation tumescence conception and birth, and death did not even exist" (327). The metaphors condense such oppositions as the lifeless and the living, the man-made and the natural, and dissolution and birth. Here there is no death; instead, all things, even the gifts Ike brings to Sam's spirit, dissolve and are "translated into the myriad life" of the wilderness, where the mythic cycles run through the days and the seasons of this life and through the hunts of the life-in-death. Ike attains the fullest vision of mythic unity on

> the knoll which was no abode of the dead because there was no death, not Lion and not Sam: not held fast in earth but free in earth and not in earth but of earth, myriad yet undiffused of every myriad part, leaf and twig and particle, air and sun and rain and dew and night, acorn oak and leaf and acorn again, dark and dawn and dark and dawn again in their immutable progression and, being myriad, one. (328–29)

But Ike has not stopped there in myth. He has walked down from the knoll and back into history. Against his vision of eternal life the narrative immediately juxtaposes an image of death, a rattlesnake. That image calls to mind the earlier metaphor of the train as snake, a passage that contrasted the train with the wilderness. Here, though, the wilderness is congruent with the snake, which lives in the woods and is marked in "a monotone concordant too with the wilderness" (329). As the snake glides away without harming Ike, he salutes it "without premeditation," as Sam had spoken to the visionary deer: "Chief. Grandfather" (330). The act carries paradoxical meanings. Sam was saluting a spirit; Ike, an animal. The visionary deer proved that a man alone in the wilderness is not isolated from other beings but can participate in the life-in-death; the rattlesnake, "evocative . . . of pariah-hood and of death," embodies death-in-life. Yet the snake is also "the old one," one of the old ancestors, and so worthy too of a salute (329).

Part 5 of "The Bear" then moves immediately to its final scene, which confronts the reader with enigmatic actions. Boon is sitting beneath the gum tree where squirrels are swarming. Why is he hammering his gun's barrel against its breech? Why is he "queerly hysterical" (330) as he hammers with "the frantic abandon of a madman" (331)? Why doesn't he look up to see who is approaching? What does he mean when he shouts, "Get out of here! Dont touch them! Dont touch a one of them! They're mine!" (331)? Is he repairing his gun or destroying it? Does he claim to own or desire to hold? Is he planning to kill the squirrels or trying to protect them? Such questions, though much debated, remain unsettled. The debates have ended inconclusively because the narrative, which has consistently blocked resolution into either juxtaposition or condensation, here resists it once more. It does so by offering copious evidence to support each alternative, and any reader can run through chains of argument. Is Boon protecting the squirrels? His sitting at the base of the gum tree reminds us of the earlier scene in which he and Ash protected the treed bear. Yet it was Boon who killed Old Ben. On the other hand, Boon killed the Bear in trying to protect Lion. Still, Boon helped train Lion, whose function was to bay the Bear so that hunters might kill it. And so on. Another argument might stem from the question of whether Boon was qualified to hold the wilderness. Was he an heir of Sam's as Ike was? Cass suggests that Boon, who had Indian blood, was a "co-heir" (300). But was Boon Sam's initiate; was he even a hunter or anything more than Sam's huntsman? His incompetence with firearms was proverbial. He did kill the Bear, but with a knife. In doing so, however, he was no skillful hunter but merely an instrument in the ritual suicide; and since Sam's death Boon has been working for the lumber company itself, an occupation that might discredit him as an heir. If it does, however, why isn't Ike also disqualified by being a carpenter? The narrative appears to intend to leave such questions unanswerable.

This enigmatic ending of "The Bear" suits the patterns of *Go Down, Moses*. The text so far has kept itself open. To stymie the reader's efforts to achieve neat resolutions, the text has, first of all, shattered chronology, and not in ways such as flashbacks that clarify but in ways that confuse or even deceive. It has alluded familiarly to acts long before recounting them, and it has presented effects before causes. Furthermore, it has offered misleading interpretations of actions and motive, postponing more accurate ones so long that only a re-reader is likely to bring the passages together. Finally, the narrative puzzles us by implying links that do not exist and concealing in all its intricacy the links that actually hold it together. These links are, on the surface, the patterns of narration (the voices in the narrative chorus), the patterns of action (rituals, plots, the fabula, and history), and the patterns of meaning (the motifs). These patterns condense from time to time into themes. On a level below those patterns run the deeper ones formed when the pairs of opposites, juxtaposition/condensation and static/dynamic, interact. Thus beneath the patterns of action are the dynamic patterns of juxtaposition—the linear $X \to Y \to Z$ of ritual, plot, fabula, and history—and of condensation, the cyclic $X \to Y \to X$ of myth. "The Bear," like the rest of *Go Down, Moses* so far, has affirmed, even stressed, both patterns although they oppose each other. Beneath the patterns of meaning are the static patterns of juxtaposition, X/Y, and of condensation, $X = Y$. Again, "The Bear" has emphasized both despite their opposing one another. Consequently, at the deepest level, beneath all the patterns and especially beneath that of theme, is the pattern of paradox. Thus in its parts—in the confrontation at the gum tree, in Part 5 itself, and in "The Bear" as a whole—as well as in all of *Go Down, Moses* up to this point, the narrative condenses juxtaposed acts and motifs and holds them together to form the theme of a union that is paradoxical.

6 / "Delta Autumn"

In "Delta Autumn" the narrative of *Go Down, Moses* returns to its "present," the year 1941, the approximate time of the opening of "Was." Once more we hear that the young men called Ike "Uncle" and that he told no one how near eighty he was. Forty-six years have passed since the latest event in "The Bear" and since Ike set out to try to free himself from responsibility and suffering by repudiating his McCaslin heritage. The passage of that time lets us judge the consequences of Ike's choices and acts in "The Bear."

"Delta Autumn" places Ike in the wilderness to which he has dedicated himself. This is the sixty-fifth time he has joined the hunt that begins by ritual in the last week of November. He remains the master woodsman. He hunts with men whom he taught in their boyhood as Sam had taught him, and he "still shot almost as well as he ever had, still killed almost as much of the game he saw as he ever killed" (336). Almost, almost. The years have left their mark, perhaps more of a mark than is acknowledged by Ike's voice and the narrator's in duet. The Big Woods where the Bear lived is gone, and for more than fifty years Ike and the other hunters have had to go all the way to the Delta to find wilderness at all, and each year further into the Delta at that. The game is scarcer, and the hunters' attitudes have changed:

> There had been bear then. A man shot a doe or a fawn as
> quickly as he did a buck, and in the afternoons they shot wild

turkey with pistols to test their stalking skill and marksman-
ship, feeding all but the breast to the dogs. (335)

No bears now survive. The deer are scarce, and so the
ritual has come to forbid killing does or fawns.

In "Delta Autumn" doe-hunting is more than an act
tabooed in the ritual. The characters use doe-hunting as a
metaphor by which to conceive of and evaluate Roth's
actions. While driving Ike and Will Legate to the Delta,
Roth slams on his car's brakes without warning and then
drives on without explanation or apology. He offers instead what seems a non sequitur: "I didn't intend to come
back in here this time." Ike protests that it is late for Roth
to change his mind, but Legate says:

> "Oh, Roth's coming. . . . If it was just a buck he was coming
> all this distance for, now. But he's got a doe in here." (337)

His words introduce the major action of "Delta Autumn":
Roth's affair. The narrative, as usual, delays our understanding of the action by deformation of the fabula:

Fabula of "Delta Autumn"

Date	Act	Position in Narrative
1879	Ike shot his first deer.	5 pp. 350–51
1881	At fourteen Ike believed that he could cure the wrong and eradicate the shame he had learned of.	6 p. 351
1888 and after	At twenty-one Ike knew he could not cure the wrong or eradicate the shame but could repudiate them "at least in principle, and at least the land itself in fact. . . ." He thought he could repudiate it for his son but found that, in repudiating it, he had lost his son.	7 pp. 351–52
1940	Box of food lost overboard. Roth went to town for supplies. When he returned, "something had happened to him."	3 pp. 337–38

Date	Act	Position in Narrative
1941: Jan.	Roth "running a doe."	2 p. 337
1941: Jan.	He and the woman go to New Mexico.	9 pp. 358–59
1941: Oct.	She has Roth's child and tells him of its birth.	10 p. 359
1941: Nov.	Ike, Roth, and the others go hunting. Roth sees the woman.	1 pp. 335–37
1941: Nov.	The hunters discuss the Depression and the approaching war. Ike's memories. Trip to camp. The hunters argue.	4 pp. 338–50
1941: Nov.	Ike thinks that he and the wilderness are coeval. The younger men go hunting. Roth leaves the envelope for the woman. Ike meets her.	8 pp. 352–58
1941: Nov.	She traces the McCaslin family and accuses Ike, Lucas, and Molly of spoiling Roth by giving him the land. She is James Beauchamp's granddaughter.	11 pp. 359–65
1941: Nov.	The younger hunters kill a deer, maybe a doe.	12 pp. 366–67

The deformations have several effects. They enable "Delta Autumn" to frame itself with the hunt by opening with the entrance into the wilderness and ending with the killing of the first game. The deformations also group the major scenes of the action, placing the introduction to Roth's "doe-hunting" just after the opening and putting the denouement just before the end. In the middle of the story stand the scene of the suppertime debate and Ike's recollections of his initiation. These form the thematic core of "Delta Autumn."

Legate's words bring to the story many of the motifs familiar from earlier in the text, the motifs of age, sex, and race:

> "Of course a old man like Uncle Ike cant be interested in no doe, not one that walks on two legs—when she's standing up, that is. Pretty light-colored, too. The one he was after them nights last fall when he said he was coon-hunting, Un-

cle Ike. The one I figured maybe he was still running when he
was gone all that month last January." (337)

What Legate says reminds Ike of how Roth had gone to
town for supplies during the previous year's hunt and
stayed overnight. "And when he did return, something
had happened to him. He would go into the woods with
his rifle each dawn when the others went, but the old
man, watching him, knew that he was not hunting" (338).
As Legate spoke, Ike watched Roth's, his kinsman's, face,
in which he discerns the lineaments of Carothers McCaslin. The observation makes explicit the motif of the family;
Ike sees, as we do, deep flaws in Roth's character. He is
sullen, brooding, a little ruthless. But what more can Ike
see? How reliable an observer is he? In the ritual tragedy
of the Bear's death Ike's final role was that of audience
rather than actor, witness rather than participant. His relinquishment itself was his attempt to withdraw from the
cast of his family's drama and from history's and to become its audience. Yet the text throws doubt on his relia-
bility as a witness by, first, using contraries to describe his
power of vision: "The eyes behind the spectacles were the
blurred eyes of an old man, but they were quite sharp too;
eyes which could still see a gun-barrel and what ran beyond it as well as any of them could" (337). Can he see
much more than that? Although Ike takes considerable
interest in Roth, who learned to hunt under his tutelage,
who is his distant cousin, and who now owns the McCaslin farm, Ike for all his watching never comprehended last
year what was going on. And in the car Ike fails to grasp
the racial connotations of Legate's words "light-colored"
and "coon-hunting." Ike's vision is blurred, and so his
testimony as a witness cannot be trusted.

    At this point, having introduced the ritual of hunting
and the motifs of the vanishing wilderness and of family,
age, sex, and race, "Delta Autumn" holds them in suspen-
sion while bringing in other motifs and indicating that
Ike's vision may be blurred by his naiveté and innocent

optimism. These effects are achieved as the narrative opens itself up to recent history and current events to a degree unmatched anywhere else in *Go Down, Moses*. All three men see that their hunts for deer or even does may be mere interludes in the broader acts of history, the Depression that has been tormenting the nation for more than a decade and the war that they feel is coming. Roth has seen Hitler come to power and expects a dictator to arise in America too. Legate is confident: "We'll stop him in this country." Roth doubts it, but Ike assures him that the Civil War and World War I proved that the nation "is a little mite stronger than any one man or group of men, outside of it or even inside of it either" (338). His words do not quench Roth's pessimism, and Legate tries to divert the talk back to hunting: "We got a deer camp—if we ever get to it. . . . Not to mention does." Refusing to be sidetracked, Ike says:

> "It's a good time to mention does. . . . Does and fawns both. The only fighting anywhere that ever had anything of God's blessing on it has been when men fought to protect does and fawns." (339)

Roth disputes that and also expresses his doubt that age has brought Ike wisdom. "Haven't you discovered in—how many years more than seventy is it?—that women and children are one thing there's never any scarcity of?" (339). Ike lets the argument end there.

The narrative next reverts to its opening motif, the vanishing wilderness. As the car travels on, Ike remembers the changes he has seen in the Delta—the wilderness transformed into cotton patches, then fields, and then plantations; the trails made by deer and bear turned into roads and then highways, settlements into towns. The panther's cries have given way to the hooting of locomotives, and not only have the animals vanished but also the Indians, memorialized now just by names and by mounds that "sepulchre their fathers' bones" (341). Memory seems

to reverse the linear flow of time, retreating "not in min-
utes . . . but in years, decades, back toward what it had
been when he first knew it" (341). When the road ends,
the hunters board a boat for the last leg of their trip to the
camp site. The boat seems to Ike to carry them back
through time to the "wilderness as he remembered it," yet
a wilderness

> now . . . two hundred miles from Jefferson when once it had
> been thirty. He had watched it, not being conquered, de-
> stroyed, so much as retreating since its purpose was served
> now and its time an outmoded time. (343)

In the conversation at supper the narrative resumes the
criticism of Roth and Ike. The talk starts where Ike's
memories had left off, with the hunters juxtaposing the
old days against the new: "Times are different now. . . .
There was game here then." Legate offers a comparison as
a gibe at Roth: "Besides, they shot does then too. . . . As it
is now, we aint got but one doe-hunter in—." Roth interrupts with a cynical and self-deprecating "And better men
hunted it. . . . Go on. Say it." Ike, with his characteristic
optimism even in the face of the Depression and the war,
disclaims such devolutionary pessimism:

> "I didn't say that. . . . There are good men everywhere, at
> all times. Most men are. Some are just unlucky, because most
> men are a little better than their circumstances give them a
> chance to be. And I've known some that even the circum-
> stances couldn't stop." (345)

Roth's response, which picks up the motif of age from the
narrator's "old man" in that passage, is brutal:

> "So you've lived almost eighty years. . . . And that's what
> you finally learned about the other animals you lived among.
> I suppose the question to ask you is, where have you been all
> the time you were dead?" (345)

While Ike merely continues the discussion as if oblivious to Roth's question, the word "dead" scandalizes the other hunters. The narration itself neither ignores the word nor is shocked by it but calls Ike's voice as he goes on talking "still peaceful and untroubled and merely grave" (346). The first four words could describe a corpse, and the last is a faint pun. The passage is, as we shall see, a part of the text's judgment of Ike; but before considering his failures, we should note his successes. He has attained much of what he sought in relinquishing the farm. Cass and his descendants have borne the responsibility for the farm. Except when hunting, Ike lives in the house his wife left him, the house that "Was" said he is "holding" for her sister (niece, the text says here). But the hunters' dwelling, either the house at de Spain's camp or the tents they have pitched for nearly fifty years since de Spain sold the Big Woods, has become his actual home. The wilderness has become "his land, although he had never owned a foot of it" (353), and he identifies himself with the wilderness:

> It belonged to all; they had only to use it well, humbly and with pride. Then suddenly he knew why he had never wanted to own any of it, arrest at least that much of what people called progress, measure his longevity at least against that much of its ultimate fate. It was because there was just exactly enough of it. He seemed to see the two of them— himself and the wilderness—as coevals. . . .

That identification leads him to another vision of the life-in-death. In his sleep he sees

> the two spans running out together, not toward oblivion, nothingness, but into a dimension free of both time and space where once more the untreed land . . . would find ample room for both— . . . the old men he had known and loved and for a little while outlived, moving again among the shades of tall unaxed trees and sightless brakes where the wild strong immortal game ran forever before the tireless belling immortal

hounds, falling and rising phoenix-like to the soundless guns.
(354)

His equating himself with the wilderness, with its "out-
moded time," makes him disgusted with "what people
called progress." Thinking that God shares his disgust, Ike
delivers what he believes to be God's judgment: "The
woods and fields [man] ravages and the game he devas-
tates will be the consequence and signature of his crime
and guilt, and his punishment" (349).

At least on the surface, Ike seems to have gained his
ends—escape from his farm, his family, and his society
into the wilderness, and escape from the responsibility
and suffering of this life into the painlessness of the life-in-
death. His initiation had marked him, prepared him, for
that and, as the text ominously says, "for more than that."
The day of his initiation led to his reading the ledgers, to
the discussion in the commissary, to the relinquishment,
and to the sterility of his marriage, all scenes that "Delta
Autumn" recapitulates here:

> that day and himself and McCaslin juxtaposed not against the
> wilderness but against the tamed land, the old wrong and
> shame itself, in repudiation and denial at least of the land and
> the wrong and shame even if he couldn't cure the wrong and
> eradicate the shame, who at fourteen when he learned of it
> had believed he could do both when he became competent
> and when at twenty-one he became competent he knew that
> he could do neither but at least he could repudiate the wrong
> and shame, at least in principle, and at least the land itself in
> fact, for his son at least: and did, thought he had: then (mar-
> ried then) . . . himself and his wife juxtaposed in their turn
> against that same land, that same wrong and shame from
> whose regret and grief he would at least save and free his son
> and, saving and freeing his son, lost him. (351)

Ike's wife loved him, the narrative assures us. Yet her love
for property was stronger; and in refusing to reclaim the

farm, Ike lost her because "women hope for so much. They never live too long to still believe that anything within the scope of their passionate wanting is likewise within the range of their passionate hope" (352). In trying to free himself and the son he hoped for from the sins of possession, Ike lost his chance to have a family of his own. Since the day of his initiation, life has brought him failed hopes, sterility, and isolation. His flight has left him in a state about which the narrative speaks only in images. Human beings are free of responsibility and suffering only in the womb and in the grave; and both sets of imagery are used, sometimes almost at once, to describe Ike. Roth's brutal question introduces the motif of death, and the narrative employs both motifs when Ike lies on his bed like a corpse, "on his back, his hands crossed on his breast and his eyes closed," and then opens his eyes and lies "peaceful and quiet as a child, looking up at the motionless belly of rain-murmured canvas," the tent that shelters him like a womb (350). He sees his own posture as deathlike when he wishes for Roth to lie awake as he himself is doing. Roth, Ike thinks, "will lie still some day for a long time without even dissatisfaction to disturb him" (353). Such images again assert motifs that support the narrative's thematic judgment on Ike: his choices have left him a "boy innocent" like Hubert Beauchamp (306), and his quest for the life-in-death has led him instead to a death-in-life.

Life, however, seems to refuse to leave him isolated, in limbo. Even without a family of his own Ike is not free of family ties. He still lives with some of his relatives and has hunted all his life with others as he now hunts with Roth. Ike's reaction to Legate's remarks about Roth shows Ike's concern for his young kinsman; and when Roth drops the envelope full of money on Ike's bed and tells him to give it to a woman and say "No," Ike clearly finds Roth reprehensible. Ike, his voice carrying the authority of "more than the blood kinsman, more even than the senior in years," commands him to wait and says:

"Will Legate was right. This is what you called coon-hunting.
And now this. . . . What did you promise her that you haven't
the courage to face her and retract?" (356)

Although Ike repeats Legate's word "coon-hunting," he
still has not grasped its implications. Imagining himself
free of the family's heritage, he cannot recognize the signs
of the repeating pattern of miscegenation, much less that
of incest; nor can he foresee that he will once again be
compelled to bear the burden of that heritage.

The meeting between Ike and the woman brings back
rituals and motifs already used in "Delta Autumn" and
employs new ones, too. Her arrival is part of a hunt in
which Roth is the quarry. With a hunting metaphor Ike
tells her, "You wont jump him here" (357). Knowing her
to have been Roth's mistress, Ike understands that the
"blanket-swaddled bundle" she carries is Roth's child and
therefore a member of the family. Ike cannot, of course,
imagine at this moment how much a member of the family
the child is; and so he perceives no significance in her
staring at him and then saying, "You're Uncle Isaac." His
questions elicit the story of her affair with Roth: their six
weeks in New Mexico, their agreement to separate, the
money he sent anonymously to a bank in Vicksburg for
her support, and the birth of their baby. She apparently
had agreed to separate only to have discovered that she
might have wanted their relationship to continue. She
was, as she says over and over again, "not sure"; yet each
time she wrote to Roth, he answered "No." "I was waiting
beside the road yesterday when your car passed," she tells
Ike, "and he saw me and so I was sure." If she has lost
interest in Roth, why has she come to the camp, Ike wonders. "What do you want?" he asks. He knows that she is
not trying to extort money from Roth. She had opened his
envelope, tilted the sheaf of banknotes onto the bed,
looked into the empty envelope, crumpled and dropped
it, and said, "That's just money." Recognizing that she
does not seek possessions, Ike repeats his question; and

when she answers, the voice of the McCaslin family, which never speaks along with Ike's voice in "Delta Autumn," speaks with hers:

> "His great great—Wait a minute.—great great *great* grandfather was your grandfather. McCaslin. Only it got to be Edmonds. Only it got to be more than that. Your cousin McCaslin was there that day when your father and Uncle Buddy won Tennie from Mr Beauchamp for the one that had no name but Terrel so you called him Tomey's Terrel, to marry. But after that it got to be Edmonds." (359)

While Ike is old and metaphorically dead, the woman, despite the "dead and toneless pallor" of her face, seems to him "young and incredibly and even ineradicably alive" (360). She has found, he feels, even in this life something of the immortality he has sought. Oblivious to him, she goes on talking, musing. "I would have made a man of him," she says. "He's not a man yet." And then she accuses Ike of having "spoiled" Roth, his pupil, kinsman, and heir. "You spoiled him. You, and Uncle Lucas and Aunt Mollie. But mostly you." Ike is astonished. "Me?" he says. "Me?" And again the voice of the McCaslins speaks, accusing him of having tried to shuffle off his own heritage, his land and his family and the burdens that accompany them. "Yes," the woman says. "When you gave to his grandfather that land which didn't belong to him, not even half of it by will or even law."

Ike defends himself by questioning her background, and finally, in the full of his blindness, blurts out the question "Haven't you got any folks at all?" When she mentions an aunt who takes in washing, Ike says, "Took in what? Took in washing?" and springs up, thinking, *"Maybe in a thousand or two thousand years in America. But not now! Not now!"* and cries, "not loud, in a voice of amazement, pity, and outrage: 'You're a nigger!' " He had been blind to clue upon clue, not only to Legate's words but also to the trip to New Mexico instead of some place closer like Memphis, to Isham's sending a young black to announce her, to her reference to what Roth's "code I suppose he would call it would forbid him forever to do" (358), to her "pallor," and finally to her naming Lucas and Molly uncle and aunt. Her reply, of course, is a still greater shock:

> "Yes. . . . James Beauchamp—you called him Tennie's Jim though he had a name—was my grandfather. I said you were Uncle Isaac." (361)

Her words are an illumination for Ike. He sees his family's heritage of miscegenation and incest renewed. In Roth's deeds as well as his visage old Carothers McCaslin endures. At this point in the narrative, however, readers can share all these perceptions with Ike and yet can stand in a position far removed from his. For them the miscegenation, even when bordering on incest, may be no outrage. Moreover, the woman's actions carry a bit of poetic justice. When old Carothers seduced Tomasina, she doubtless believed her father to be her mother's husband Thucydus; but Carothers surely knew that she was his own child. Yet he must not have cared until Eunice's suicide compelled him to regard Tomasina as a daughter rather than a possession, just as Lucas warned that his suicide would leave Zack "something to think about" or as Rider's death left the deputy puzzled. Here in "Delta Autumn," however, it is the "black" woman, not the white man, who knows what the seduction means and does not mind that meaning. She has the autonomy that has earned her the right to say that she and only she could have made Roth a man. She knows and accepts her family, even the white branches of it, and stands above the dread of her heritage—of her family's history and, as her ignoring the money suggests, of mankind's guilt of the sins of possession. Although Ike now understands that she did not come to meet Roth or to get money, he never quite grasps what brought her to the camp. She came to see him. The ties of the family drew her to meet "Uncle Ike" and to announce the existence of her line of the family that runs back through James Beauchamp and Turl to Tomasina and Carothers McCaslin. Although she and the family are bound together, she is free of the McCaslin land and of the restrictions of Southern culture and the family's own somewhat less narrow racial attitudes. "I'm going back North," she says. "Back home" (361).

In his outrage Ike burns to expel her. "Get out of here!" he cries. "I can do nothing for you! Cant nobody do nothing for you!" As she starts to leave, he calls, "Wait," and sets the banknotes where she can reach them. When she merely looks at them blankly and without interest, Ike grows frantic. In a rapture of disgust at all that the money represents, he implores her in the tones of perhaps an endangered virgin, "Take it out of my tent" (362). The money and the affair threaten to stain the purity that Ike imagines he has acquired, and in the broadest sense the acts of his kin are compelling him to recognize that his heritage confines and even defines him.

As she picks up the banknotes, however, contrary feeling arise in Ike. Again calling, "Wait," he puts out his hand to her; and she in response reaches out to him until he can touch her hand; and with that touch a cycle completes itself.

> He didn't grasp it, he merely touched it—the gnarled, blood-less, bone-light bone-dry old man's fingers touching for a second the smooth young flesh where the strong old blood ran after its long lost journey back to home. "Tennie's Jim," he said. "Tennie's Jim." (362)

That touch joins McCaslin with McCaslin. The "man-made" lines of the family come together; and their condensation, though momentary, joins once again—here at the latest as at the beginning of the family's genealogy—

youth and age, "black" and white, woman and man, the possessed and the possessor.

The thematic significance of that touch resembles the significance of the baby. In Roth's and the woman's son, family lines also condense. He unites the illegitimate and the legitimate, the "black" and the white, the possessed and the possessor, the "man-made" line that stems from Turl and the "woman-made" one from Mary McCaslin Edmonds, the sister of Buck and Buddy. Although the boy descends from the white Edmondses and the "black" Beauchamps, there remains one line from which he has inherited nothing: the white McCaslin line that will die out with Ike. Consequently, when Ike for the third time calls to the woman to wait and asks her to take down from its hook his hunting-horn, his act has deep thematic import. Saying, "It's his. Take it," Ike bequeaths the horn to the little boy, thereby making him heir to the wilderness, the inheritance that Ike had accepted from Sam and through him from "the old free fathers" whom Ike described in "The Bear" as the direct ancestors of blacks because blacks were not sullied, as even Indians were, by the sin of possession.

Yet Ike is incapable of maintaining this stance and reverses his position again. His voice "running away with him," he launches into a diatribe. "That's right," he says. "Go back North. Marry: a man in your own race. That's the only salvation for you—for a while yet, maybe a long while yet. We will have to wait" (363). The "We" comes as a surprise. If his remarks were as racist as they first sound, his pronoun would have been "you." The word *salvation* carries almost religious connotations for Ike here. He is advising the woman on how he thinks she can be saved from the sin of possession. She must flee from whites, from the South, from the McCaslin family, and from Roth. "We"—that is, white Southerners in general and McCaslins in particular—must stay behind to bear the guilt a while longer. That notion may recall what Ike said to Fonsiba's husband in the cabin in Arkansas:

"Granted that my people brought the curse onto the land: maybe for that reason their descendants alone can—not resist it, not combat it—maybe just endure and outlast it until the curse is lifted. Then your peoples' turn will come because we have forfeited ours. But not now. Not yet." (278)

His diatribe, as it goes on, becomes both racist and blindly insensitive. He tells her to find a black man whom she can treat as Roth has treated her:

"You are young, handsome, almost white; you could find a black man who would see in you what it was you saw in him [Roth], who would ask nothing of you and expect less and get even still less than that, if it's revenge you want. Then you will forget all this, forget it ever happened, that he ever existed—" (363)

Ike's advice is not only heartless but also mindless. He is recommending an impossibility. For her to devote her life to "revenge" for Roth's acts and at the same time to expect to "forget all this" would be a contradiction. Ike fully deserves the rebuke he gets. After an instant in which "she blazed silently down at him" in what must have been, in her turn, amazement, pity, and outrage, she says to him quietly, "Old man, have you lived so long and forgotten so much that you dont remember anything you ever knew or felt or even heard about love?" (363). The answer, unspoken in the narrative, would have to be yes.

Falling back in his bed, his usual optimism shattered, Ike silently spews out a jeremiad in which his ideals and his prejudices tumble over one another, his love for the land and his sympathy for the dispossessed clashing with his racism, his naive tendency to abstract and over-simplify societal relationships, and his hitherto unspoken lust for the apocalypse:

This Delta. *This land which man has deswamped and denuded and deriverd in two generations so that white men can own plantations and commute every night to Memphis and black men own planta-*

tions and ride in jim crow cars to Chicago to live in millionaires'
mansions on Lakeshore Drive, where white men rent farms and live
like niggers and niggers crop on shares and live like animals, where
cotton is planted and grows man-tall in the very cracks of the side-
walks, and usury and mortgage and bankruptcy and measureless
wealth, Chinese and African and Aryan and Jew, all breed and
spawn together until no man has time to say which one is which nor
cares. . . . No wonder the ruined woods I used to know dont
cry for retribution! he thought: The people who have destroyed it will accomplish its revenge. (364)

After that passage "Delta Autumn" comes quickly to an
end. Legate enters the tent to look for a knife and reports
that Roth has slain a deer. When Ike asks, "what was
it?"—that is, was it a doe?—Legate implies that it was not.
"Just a deer," he says. "Nothing extra." His last phrase
indicates that it was a buck with no exceptional antlers. Ike
then lies back down in the posture of a corpse and says to
himself, "It was a doe." While he may mean that literally,
he surely means it figuratively. To him Roth seems to have
ruined the woman's life in a way enough like the way
Carothers ruined Eunice's to bring Ike to despair. Ike sees
his life, his quest, as a failure and therefore as irony. To
him the McCaslins appear doomed to repeat the cycle of
their history. Looking at Roth, Ike believes himself to have
set an example that no one has followed. His family and
his society seem dominated by their heritage of guilt as
strongly as ever. From Ike's viewpoint history itself is not
a line of progress but a cycle of imprisonment.

Yet Ike in his blindness despairs when despair is useless
and not wholly appropriate. However much Roth resembles Carothers, they are not identical. As we can recall
from Roth's relationships with Lucas, Molly, and Henry in
"The Fire and the Hearth," he has been in the words of
"Delta Autumn" itself "tempered a little, altered a little"
(337). While Carothers was ruthless or at best callously
thoughtless until Eunice's suicide gave him something to
think about, Roth is less callous and is tolerant although
cynical. His cynicism itself derives from his constant

awareness of his own shortcomings. They pained him after he forced his playmate Henry to assume the role of subordinate, when in recompense Lucas and Molly made Roth eat alone at their table and he ate the "bitter fruit" of his heritage, and whenever he found himself in contention with Lucas. Roth's most recent contemptuous judgment upon himself followed Ike's rambling assertion that

> "I think that every man and woman, at the instant when it dont even matter whether they marry or not, I think that whether they marry then or afterward or dont never, at that instant the two of them together were God."

Ike's principle, whatever it means, turns out to be one that he is manifestly unwilling to apply to Roth and the woman when he learns of their affair. Roth rejects it too.

> "Then there are some Gods in this world I wouldn't want to touch, and with a damn long stick. . . . And that includes myself. (348)

Roth is no ideal, but he is a better man than Ike can give him credit for. He is following Cass's path, not Ike's, by remaining immersed in the turmoil of this world rather than trying to flee to a probably unattainable state of primal purity. Like every other man, Roth has had to eat the fruit of his heritage. His cynicism toward himself as well as others signifies that he knows the bitterness of its taste; but he does not pretend, as Ike does, that he has rinsed that bitterness away.

Ike need not despair over the woman either. She combines Tomasina's willingness with Eunice's strength of mind and independence of action. In having an affair with her, Roth has not destroyed her. He has not killed that doe. On the contrary, she has the power to dominate him. She is the hunter; Roth, who fled into the woods at her approach, is the quarry. She can offer love and, when Roth proves unworthy, withdraw it. Innocent of the sins of possession, she has reached something like the spiritual life that Ike thought existed only in the life-in-death: she seems to him "ineradicably alive." She has achieved a freedom of movement within the family, between the races, and across regional boundaries that no other McCaslin has attained. She seems able to gamble and lose and play again. The two McCaslin men conceive of themselves as moving through ironic patterns of action and meaning; but the woman and her son, in whom are united the lines of the family and the motifs of opposition and possession, imply the comic pattern in which an old, rigid, and imprisoning society gives way to a youthful, flexible, free society that enhances the possibilities of life. The woman and, through her, the boy seem likely to endure and maybe even to prevail.

7 / "Go Down, Moses"

In the final story of the book the narrative withdraws from the wilderness and, as in "Pantaloon in Black," seems to attentuate its connections with the McCaslin family and the farm. The first of the story's two sections starts with the third-person narrator's portrait of a hip young black man whose eyes have "seen too much." Dressed in an "ensemble" of matching shirt and trousers that "had cost too much and were draped too much, with too many pleats," he is lying on a cot in a prison cell awaiting his execution; and in a voice that was "anything under the sun but a southern voice or even a negro voice" (369), he is answering the questions of a young white man who is taking the census. When the prisoner identifies himself as "Samuel Worsham Beauchamp. Twenty-six. Born in the country near Jefferson, Mississippi," he links the story to the book's narrative.

Samuel is cool. He has exposed his alias and thereby startled the census-taker, who blurts out, "That's not the name you were sen—lived under in Chicago." Samuel snaps the ash from his cigarette and says, "No. It was another guy killed the cop" (369).

> "All right. Occupation—
> "Getting rich too fast.
> —none." . . . "Parents."
> "Sure. Two. I dont remember them. My grandmother raised me."
> "What's her name? Is she still living?"

"I dont know. Mollie* Worsham Beauchamp. If she is, she's
on Carothers Edmonds' farm seventeen miles from Jefferson,
Mississippi." (370)

The census-taker, finished, stands up. He is younger and
has seen less and, touched by Samuel's plight, asks, "If
they dont know who you are here, how will they know—
how do you expect to get home?" Samuel continues playing it cool, snapping off the ash again and saying, "What
will that matter to me?" He keeps smoking until he is led
out that evening to his death, and the section ends. Despite his bravado, however, Samuel does care about being
buried by his family and in native ground. Getting
"home" does matter; and as the other part of the story
reveals, he has already done his part to arrange his return
by telling the sympathetic young white man his identity.
    Section 2, the last part of "Go Down, Moses," tells how
Samuel's body was brought home for burial. On the morning before his execution Molly comes into Jefferson from
Roth's farm and appears in the office of the town attorney,
Gavin Stevens. When he hears her name, he connects her
with the farm; but she says, "I done left. I come to find my
boy" and then begins to chant, "Roth Edmonds sold my
Benjamin. Sold him in Egypt. Pharaoh got him." The narrative describes her objectively as "a little old negro
woman with a shrunken, incredibly old face beneath a
white headcloth and a black straw hat which would have
fitted a child." Stevens, however, calls her "Aunty." That
patronizing word should make his attitude and his judgment suspect if the narrator's description has not already
done so:

> a thin, intelligent, unstable face, a rumpled linen suit from
> whose lapel a Phi Beta Kappa key dangled on a watch chain—
> Gavin Stevens, Phi Beta Kappa, Harvard, Ph.D. Heidelberg,

---

*Throughout "Go Down, Moses" her name is spelled "Mollie" rather than
"Molly."

whose office was his hobby, although it made his living for him, and whose serious vocation was a twenty-two-year-old unfinished translation of the Old Testament back into classic Greek. (370–71)

Besides the "Aunty," Stevens's words in many other instances reveal the racism that underlies his complacent liberalism. One example may be his often calling Molly a "Negress" in the narrative's free indirect discourse. In direct quotations he certainly calls her "nigger" and calls blacks "darkies." Even in 1941 those two words were in poor taste among upper-class and even middle-class Southerners.

Molly's arrival puzzles Stevens. "If you dont know where your grandson is," he asks, "how do you know he's in trouble?" She repeats, "It was Roth Edmonds sold him. . . . Sold him in Egypt. I dont know whar he is. I just knows Pharaoh got him. And you the Law. I wants to find my boy" (371). Here as at the end of "The Fire and the Hearth" Molly has the power of a seer. Unerringly the old black woman senses trouble and finds the man who will help her.

As he starts considering how to look for Molly's grandson, Stevens recalls Samuel's youth. Like both Ike and Roth, Samuel had not grown up with his parents. His mother died at his birth, and he was later deserted by his father, who is now serving time in prison for manslaughter. Samuel, like Roth, was brought up by Molly and Lucas. At nineteen Samuel came to Jefferson, gambled, fought, spent some time in jail, got caught breaking into a store, assaulted the arresting officer, was jailed, broke out two nights later, and disappeared. Stevens plans to call Roth to find out what he knows; and in thinking of Roth, Stevens comes to understand Molly's chant. He remembers that Roth had caught Samuel breaking into the commissary and had ordered him off the place and forbidden him to return.

With implicit faith in Molly's power of divination, Ste-

vens seeks the best source of news. The editor of the
county papers does not need to leave his desk to hand
Stevens the wire service flimsy that answers his question:

> *Mississippi negro, on eve of execution for murder of Chicago police-
> man, exposes alias by completing census questionnaire. Samuel Wor-
> sham Beauchamp—* (374)

Although Stevens had regarded Samuel as having inherited "some seed not only violent but dangerous and
bad" (372) and had hoped his trouble would be "very bad
and maybe final" (374), Stevens is shaken by the news.
Unable to stomach any lunch, he returns to his office.

Waiting for him there is Miss Worsham. The narrative
describes her so as to emphasize two qualities. First, she
has fallen on hard times: she lives in a decaying house,
gives lessons in china-painting, and raises and sells chick-
ens and vegetables. On the other hand, she remains an
aristocratic old lady: she is strikingly erect, carries a
frayed, faded, rusty umbrella and an old-fashioned
beaded reticule, and still has the help of Hamp Worsham,
who is the descendant of one of her father's slaves and is
also Molly's brother. The narrative juxtaposes Miss Worsham's understanding of Molly against Stevens's insen-
sitivity. Miss Worsham's sympathy stems from her sharing with Molly a common background that can be
described through motifs of possession, age, heritage, and
family. Miss Worsham says:

> "Mollie's and Hamp's parents belonged to my grandfather.
> Mollie and I were born in the same month. We grew up
> together as sisters would." (375)

She has come to Stevens to see that the wishes that Molly
has not even expressed will be met. Without her Stevens
would do the best he knew, but he frequently misunder-
stands what Molly would want. He would let Samuel be
buried up North; Molly will want Samuel buried on the

farm. As Miss Worsham tells Stevens, "She will want to take him back home with her." Stevens, astonished, says, "Him?" Miss Worsham explains that Samuel "is the only child of her oldest daughter, her own dead first child. He must come home." Abashed, Stevens agrees, "He must come home. I'll attend to it at once." Miss Worsham next volunteers to defray the cost of the funeral and asks how much that would come to. "Ten or twelve dollars will cover it," Stevens says. "They will furnish a box and there will be only the transportation." Miss Worsham looks at him "as though he were a child." Both Molly's and Miss Worsham's respect for the rituals and the motifs of the family necessitate a proper funeral. "A box?" Miss Worsham says. "He is her grandson, Mr Stevens. When she took him to raise, she gave him my father's name— Samuel Worsham. Not just a box, Mr Stevens" (376). Again Stevens stands corrected. "Not just a box," he says and suggests that Roth, Lucas, and he himself could contribute the money. "That will not be necessary," Miss Worsham replies and counts out twenty-five dollars in frayed bills and in coins, even pennies. When Stevens says that Samuel "will die tonight," she replies, "I will tell her this afternoon that he is dead then." She declines Stevens's offer to be the one who tells Molly but accepts his suggestion that he go out to "talk to her" in the evening.

Stevens's ignorance of what Molly and Miss Worsham consider proper is the result of his condescension toward blacks. His paternalism prevents his treating them with respect. He does not instinctively take their feelings so seriously as he would those of whites. Yet he accepts instruction gracefully not only from Miss Worsham but also from Molly and, in arranging the funeral, carries out their wishes. Stevens tells the editor that the funeral will cost two hundred and twenty-five dollars and that the two of them will have to bear most of the cost. He says that he will get something from Roth and raise whatever he can around the square, and he spends the afternoon going from store to store. His "set speech"—"It's to bring a dead

nigger home. It's for Miss Worsham. Never mind about a
paper to sign: just give me a dollar. Or a half a dollar then.
Or a quarter then" (378–79)—expresses his own attitudes
and those of the people to whom he is appealing. The
racism is evident not only in the word "nigger" but also in
the assertion that it is being done for the white woman,
not the black. Class consciousness is evident too in the
contrast between the social implications of the words *nigger* and *Miss Worsham*. Naming the sums of money in de-
scending order shows that the townspeople's generosity is
limited. On the other hand, they do contribute, "merchant
and clerk, proprietor and employee, doctor dentist lawyer
and barber," a cross-section of the upper- and middle-
class whites in Jefferson; and in contributing, they share in
the responsibility for returning Samuel to the farm; they
help bring him home.

That night Stevens walks to Miss Worsham's "through
the breathless and star-filled darkness" (379). Those words
suggest the ritual of the vision. In "Pantaloon in Black"
and "The Old People" breathlessness was part of the
change of atmosphere that preceded visions of the spirits
of the dead, and in the latter story moments of contemplation and understanding occurred beneath the stars. Yet no
supernatural vision of Samuel's spirit occurs here. If there
is any vision, it must be one involving the natural and
familiar acts and meanings that do occur in the rest of "Go
Down, Moses." Furthermore, if there is contemplation
and understanding, it cannot be Stevens's. His acts have
been valuable, but his judgments have proved faulty over
and over again. Indeed, the narrative might deserve criticism for undercutting him so energetically if the com-
ments of Faulkner's readers did not make it plain that
even such heavy-handedness cannot prevent some critics
from identifying Stevens with Faulkner. Why do readers
place such confidence in Stevens? Is it because he went to
Harvard? Because he has a doctorate from Heidelberg?
Because he is a lawyer? Because he speaks grammatically?
Because he talks and talks? It is hard to imagine why; but

given his continual misconceptions, only the gullible would trust him to see whatever there is to be seen. The vision, if there is one, must be comprehended by someone else, by Miss Worsham, by Molly, by the blacks, or maybe only by the reader.

Miss Worsham's record for understanding is itself not faultless, as the end of the story reveals. She tells Stevens that Molly "mustn't know" how Samuel died (375), and Stevens and the editor agree to keep the story out of the newspaper. Yet, when Samuel's coffin is being taken off the train, Molly asks the editor, "Is you gonter put hit in de paper? I wants hit all in de paper. All of hit" (383). Even Miss Worsham patronizes Molly and wants to shield her from the truth. Molly, though, is not afraid of facts. In the first place, she raised Samuel, lived in the family with him for nineteen years, and saw him grow into the man he was when Roth exiled him from the farm. What Miss Worsham cannot understand is, of course, the scope of Molly's understanding: nothing is hidden from a seer.

Miss Worsham, however, is closer to the center of things than Stevens is. When he knocks on her door, he is admitted by Hamp Worsham, who descends from her family's slaves and bears her family name. Worsham invites Stevens in and directs him not to the servants' rooms, to their quarters or the kitchen, or to some prim and formal parlor, but upstairs to a bedroom, to the most private region of her house. That surprises Stevens, who asks, "Is that where Aunt Molly is?" Worsham's reply, in all its brevity, is rich with the motifs of the condensation of opposites—black and white, elder and younger, man and woman, and master and servant—within the family. "We all dar," he says.

In the bedroom Stevens finds Molly sitting beside "the hearth on which even tonight [that is, in July] a few ashes smoldered faintly" (379). Even in Miss Worsham's house the ritual fire is burning; and she and Molly and Hamp are sitting in "a circle about the brick hearth on which the ancient symbol of human coherence and solidarity smoldered" (380). Hamp's wife, whose "light" color implies the mixing of black and white, is leaning in the doorway. Stevens sits in the circle, but he does not belong there because he does not grasp what is going on. Believing that everyone wants him to talk, he starts speaking to Molly, thereby interrupting the family's ritual of mourning. She never looks at him.

> "He dead," she said, "Pharaoh got him."
> "Oh yes, Lord," Worsham said. "Pharaoh got him."
> "Done sold my Benjamin. . . . Sold him in Egypt."

Miss Worsham, not entirely at one with the ritual herself, tries to hush Hamp, and Stevens attempts to correct what he regards as Molly's misconception. "It wasn't Mr Edmonds. Mr Edmonds didn't—." Doubtless Stevens is correct enough. Roth, for all his hot-headedness and cynicism, has shown considerable patience and tolerance and respect, especially for Lucas and Molly and their family. The narrative itself supports Stevens in his effort to vindicate Roth. Except for Molly's refrain "Roth Edmonds sold my Benjamin," nothing in the narrative accuses Roth of injustice or even lack of mercy. Instead, the narrative may raise questions about how Samuel was affected by heredity—"A bad son of a bad father" (375)—and by losing his parents and by his upbringing at Molly's, where "the old woman raised him. Or where she tried to" (378). Those judgments are suspect because they are Stevens's. Yet the text has given independent evidence that Molly and Lucas are not ideal parents: they have had trouble with their daughter, Nat, and the woman in "Delta Autumn" surprisingly included them with Ike as people who had "spoiled" Roth. In the end, though, "Go Down, Moses" never says why Samuel went wrong. In offering many possible causes for his violence, the text makes every cause questionable. Nor does the text show to what extent Roth was to blame for Samuel's fate. Molly's chant cannot be taken as fact or even as allegory. It has too many loose ends for that. Benjamin was Jacob's younger son by his last wife, Rachel, who died in giving him birth; but no one ever sold Benjamin into Egypt. It was Joseph, their elder son, whom his older half-brothers did betray into captivity in Egypt. Over the years Joseph rose to be viceroy; and eventually, so the well-known story goes, a famine afflicted Canaan, and Jacob sent all his sons except his beloved Benjamin to Egypt for food. There they appealed to Joseph, whom they did not recognize. He pretended to think them spies; and they tried to vouch for their honesty by naming their father and their brother Benjamin. Pretending to test their word, Joseph ordered them to leave one brother behind, return to Canaan, and bring Benjamin back to Egypt. When Jacob heard of that command, he did bewail the necessity of sending Benjamin to Egypt but not his having been sold there. The text of "Go Down, Moses" refers to that biblical account no more than allusively. Benjamin's career resembles that of Molly's grandson only in that he is dear to her and had gone into danger far from home. The biblical analogy may fit Roth's relationship to Samuel more closely than Molly's. As Jacob mourned the necessity to send Benjamin away for the good of the family, so Roth may have regretted exiling Samuel. Still, the text does not show his regret or even prove that Samuel deserved exile but merely confirms that Roth expelled him from the farm, cut him off from the land, his home, and his family. Exile alienates Samuel from his heritage as relinquishment alienated Ike. Ike had no home but a tent to return to, and relinquishment made him metaphorically a corpse. Samuel insures his own return home even if only as a literal corpse. Consequently, unanswerable questions about Samuel's life and Roth's guilt must not distract the reader as they distract Stevens from what is actually taking place at Miss Worsham's, from the sharing in the family ritual of mourning.

Stevens himself is unable to take part in it. Seeming to feel himself drowning, he almost runs away. *"Soon I will be outside. . . . Then there will be air, space, breath"* (380–81). The

breathlessness of the visionary is not for him. As Miss
Worsham follows him to the front door, he can hear the
chanting upstairs, not only Molly and Hamp, Samuel's
bloodkin, but also his family by marriage, Hamp's wife, "a
true constant soprano which ran without words beneath
the strophe and antistrophe of the brother and sister."
Stevens apologizes to Miss Worsham: "I ask you to forgive
me. I should have known. I shouldn't have come." "It's all
right," she says; and then, including herself in the group
of proper mourners as Hamp himself had included her
with his "We all dar," she says simply, "It's our grief." In
the ritual of mourning, Samuel's family is thus extended
still further, beyond the McCaslins and the Beauchamps
and the Edmondses, beyond blood and marriage and race
toward, if only a little way toward, the communal anonymity of brotherhood.

The group of mourners and of those who do not yet
mourn, who perhaps like Stevens cannot yet mourn,
grows when Samuel's coffin is unloaded from the train.
Whites and blacks assemble, old and young, men and
women from the country and others from the town, some
mourners and some onlookers. Under the eyes of a cross-
section of society the somber ritual takes place. Not all the
blacks are deeply sympathetic. According to the narrator,
the "Negro undertaker's men" proceed with unseemly
haste. They

> snatched the wreaths and floral symbols of man's ultimate
> and inevitable end briskly out and slid the casket in and flung
> the flowers back and clapped-to the door. (382)

Then the hearse drives through town "while the mer-
chants and clerks and barbers and professional men who
had given Stevens the dollars and half-dollars and quarters and the ones who had not, watched quietly." Behind
the hearse bearing Samuel's coffin are two cars, Molly and
Miss Worsham in the first, Stevens and the editor in the

second. The narrative portrays the scene as the juxtaposition and condensation of motifs:

> the high-headed erect white woman, the old Negress, the designated paladin of justice and truth and right, the Heidelberg Ph.D.—in formal component complement to the Negro murderer's catafalque: the slain wolf. (382)

Samuel's cortege thus unites once more white and black, master and servant, man and woman, old and young, farm and town, family and outsider, hunter and quarry.

Just beyond the town line Stevens switches off the ignition of the editor's car, and it coasts to a stop. The hearse and the car that contains Samuel's "family " speed on to the farm. Stevens shows again that he can learn from experience. He will not try to take part in the burial ritual. He is still not ready to share the family's grief. The editor, while turning the car around to head back to town, tells of Molly's request that "all of hit" be put in the paper, a request that the editor, unable to share Molly's feelings, apparently will not grant. Stevens believes that he understands them:

> *It doesn't matter to her now. Since it had to be and she couldn't stop it, and now that it's all over and done and finished, she doesn't care how he died. She just wanted him home, but she wanted him to come home right. She wanted that casket and those flowers and the hearse and she wanted to ride through town behind it in a car. (383)*

Leaving aside the fact that Miss Worsham wanted the funeral as much as Molly did, Stevens makes it sound as if Molly wished for a parade in which she would be the central figure. Obviously he is wrong about that, wrong as usual, but this time not wholly wrong. Molly did want Samuel home and wanted him to come home right. She wanted him returned to his land, home, and family through the proper rituals of mourning and burial; and with some help from the townspeople in general, from the

editor, Stevens, and above all Miss Worsham, Molly has
restored her grandson to his heritage.

The events in Section 2 of "Go Down, Moses" succeed
those of the first section in chronological order so that the
story's plot and its fabula coincide except for the two-part
flashback in which Stevens recalls Samuel's past. Setting
up the fabula entails one problem not hitherto encoun-
tered in *Go Down, Moses*. The events in this story cannot be
precisely dated and then tied into the chronology of the
book. The month is July; and since a census is underway,
the year is probably 1940; but so far as I can see, there is no
way to be certain.

Fabula of "Go Down, Moses"

Date—in terms of Samuel's age	Act	Position in Narrative
Birth to 20	Samuel was orphaned at birth, deserted by his father, and raised by Molly and Lucas. At nineteen he left the farm, went to Jefferson, and spent a year in and out of jail. After his arrest for breaking and entering and assault, he was jailed, but he escaped.	3 p. 373
19	Roth caught him breaking into the commissary and exiled him from the farm.	5 p. 373
26—the eve of his execution	Samuel gives his name to the census-taker.	1 pp. 369–70
26—the day of his execution	Molly goes to Stevens for help in finding Samuel.	2 pp. 370–72
26—the day of his execution	Stevens remembers the commissary break-in and the exile.	4 p. 373
26—the day of his execution	Stevens finds the newspaper story and meets Miss Worsham. They plan the funeral. He collects money and visits the mourners.	6 pp. 373–81
26—two days later	The funeral	7 pp. 381–83

This movement away from the book's concrete chronology serves to abstract, to generalize, time by blurring without erasing the story's temporal links to the book's fabula. The fabula fits the finite dynamic pattern of juxtaposition ($X \to Y \to Z$) and is grounded in history, which follows the infinite pattern ($\ldots X \to Y \to Z \ldots$). Because of the blurring the story is enigmatically related to the fabula and yet ostensibly independent of it—ostensibly but not truly independent of the fabula as are the mythic cycles in the pattern of dynamic condensation ($X \to Y \to X$) of the life-in-death.

A similar contrast occurs at the end of *Go Down, Moses* in the settings for the action. "Go Down, Moses" has relinquished the wilderness as a setting. In the narrative, at least, Ike and the wilderness have proved coeval; he and it have vanished simultaneously from the book. The farm has receded into the background, giving way first to the city and then to the town. Wherever the book has touched upon the city, it has been presented as an alien world. In his boyhood Ike doubted that a "city-bred man . . .could comprehend loving the life he spills" (181) and found that "in Memphis it was not all right" (231). As an old man Ike sees white farmers and black sharecroppers struggling while white plantation owners commute to Memphis and black ones live in mansions in Chicago (364). Wilderness and city thus serve as the positively and negatively charged poles of the narrative, the wilderness as the lost Eden where all men were once brothers and the city as the waste land where all men are strangers. Between the polar opposites are the farm, which is adjacent to the wilderness, and the town, adjacent to the city. On the farm the communal anonymity of brotherhood is no longer possible, but men live together as a family, a society that defines and is defined by its rituals and motifs. The town is the farm generalized, the rituals and motifs of the family adopted and then adapted by a wider society. In "Go Down, Moses" the acts and feelings characteristic of families gradually pass along a continuum of the society of the town. At the source of the continuum is Molly mourning her dead grandson, her foster child, blood grieving for blood. The continuum extends through Hamp, who is in a parallel line; through his wife as a relative by marriage; through Miss Worsham, who shares in the family's heritage; and, further and further from the source, through Stevens and the editor and the townspeople at large. The four settings thus fit both the static and the dynamic patterns of juxtaposition. In the former, wilderness opposes city; and between those extremes is the mediating juxtaposition of farm and town:

WILDERNESS / farm   / /   town / CITY

The dynamic pattern also describes relationships among the four scenes. In the linear pattern of history in *Go Down, Moses* the wilderness has been giving way to the farm, farms have spawned towns, and towns have grown into cities. That pattern, however, does not imply the paving of all farmland and the transformation of America into megalopolis. Although the wilderness is withdrawing, a little can be preserved. More significant, the narrative guarantees that the farm will continue "solvent and efficient and intact and still increasing so long as McCaslin and his McCaslin successors lasted, even though their surnames might not even be Edmonds then" (298). Although at the end of *Go Down, Moses* the farm has receded, it remains the narrative's archetypal setting for human relationships, for home, family, and sharing. It signifies the rituals and motifs that may penetrate and unify the town and, someday, if the feelings and acts of the census-taker can bear this much weight, even the city. Ultimately, though, the center of interest for the narrative is not in the extremes of wilderness and city but in the mediating positions of farm and town. They are the settings for the narrative's major themes.

As *Go Down, Moses* comes to its predictably inconclusive end, no character has the power to express those themes. The more characters see, it seems, the less they talk. Nor does the narrator articulate the meaning of the narrative. The text leaves readers on their own to devise meanings adequate to the narrative. Those meanings, whatever they are, must be congruent with the patterns already seen in the text. Its pattern of narration is its weaving voices together in the narrative chorus. The patterns of action—myth, ritual, plot, fabula, and history—unify *Go Down, Moses*, too. These are the dynamic patterns: the cyclic $X \to Y \to X$ of myth; the finite linear $X \to Y \to Z$ of ritual, plot, and fabula; and the infinite linear $\ldots X \to Y \to Z \ldots$ of history. Myth is the dynamic pattern of condensation and lies beneath the narrative's emphasis on natural cycles. Myth supports rebirth—"acorn oak and leaf and acorn again" (328)—and resurrection, whether in natural terms or in biblical ones as in Molly's declaration that "God say, 'What's rendered to My earth, it belong to Me unto I resurrect it'" (102), or in terms of the life-in-death in which Mannie, the Old People, the spirit-deer, the Bear, Sam, and Lion exist in "a dimension free of both time and space" where also "the wild strong immortal game ran forever before the tireless belling immortal hounds, falling and rising phoenix-like to the soundless guns" (354).

In opposition to the dynamic condensation of myth is the dynamic juxtaposition of ritual, plot, fabula, and history. In the narrative, rituals recur, but with variations. Sam initiates Cass and Ike, and Ike initiates Roth and other young men; but each initation has, as we have seen, different consequences. The vision of Mannie and the life-in-death leads Rider to commit ritual suicide by having himself killed by means of another ritual, the lynching. The vision of the spirit-deer reveals the life-in-death to Ike. His suicide is, however, only metaphorical. The Bear's death and Sam's are also ritual suicides. The prevalence of such deaths raises suspicions that Jobaker and Samuel may have had themselves slain, but such questions cannot be resolved. Hunting, another ritual, has been a literal or metaphorical activity in almost every section of *Go Down, Moses*. Furthermore, rituals can create, preserve, and end the existence of families. In Lucas's and Molly's house, in Rider's and Mannie's, and in Miss Worsham's and Hamp's the fire burns on the hearth. The rituals of courting, seduction, marriage, divorce, death, and mourning appear throughout *Go Down, Moses*. The rituals of possession—owning, taming, sharing, holding, relinquishing, dowering, bequeathing, inheriting, expropriating, being dispossessed, being possessed, selling, buying, losing, and winning—generate much of the narrative's action. All these lines of ritual are unifying elements in *Go Down, Moses*.

Yet rituals are like threads in the book. Small-scale, finite patterns of action, they are twisted into the strands of the plots, which are finite patterns on a larger scale. While the stories in *Go Down, Moses* have plots and some parts of its stories do too, the whole of the narrative completes no pattern of action. Its inconclusiveness implies that significant acts will occur after the close of the plot. Rather than concluding the plot by bringing the action to a climax, the narrative shows a movement from holding through dispossessing, owning, taming, relinquishing, and sharing, and implies that this trend will continue until someday owners will have repaid their debts to the dispossessed. Thus plot—which traditionally ties itself up, closes itself off—remains open and points beyond itself toward the future. Such openness must stress time and therefore must emphasize the fabula, which is the finite chronological arrangement of the acts in the plot, and history, which is the infinite chronology of which the fabula is a part.

By submerging plot in fabula and fabula in history, the narrative obliges us to return to the questions that "The Bear" raised but left unsettled. The first of these asked whether the pattern of history is a circle or a line. *Go Down, Moses* has intimated that the pattern is both, and the book's title supports the paradoxical assertion of simultaneous linearity and circularity by alluding to the spiritual "Go Down, Moses." The spiritual must occur in

many versions, but here is the well-known one that James
Weldon Johnson chose for *The Book of American Negro Spirituals* in 1923:

> Go down, Moses,
>   'Way down in Egypt land,
> Tell ole Pharaoh,
>   To let my people go.
> Go down, Moses,
>   'Way down in Egypt land,
> Tell ole Pharaoh,
>   To let my people go.
> When Israel was in Egypts land:
>   Let my people go,
> Oppressed so hard they could not stand,
>   Let my people go.
>
> "Thus spoke the Lord," bold Moses said;
>   Let my people go,
> If not I'll smite your first born dead,
>   Let my people go.
>
> Go Down, Moses,
>   'Way down in Egypt land,
> Tell ole Pharaoh,
>   To let my people go.
> O let my people go.

The spiritual refers to the biblical scene in which God
orders Moses to try to free the Israelites from bondage in
Egypt. Now there is no allegorical relationship, no chain
of one-to-one correspondences, between *Go Down, Moses*
and either the spiritual or the biblical story. At most there
are analogies. Yet since no critic so far as I know has dis-
cussed the relevance of the allusions in more than general
terms, it is worthwhile to explore the analogies.

The acts and meanings of the scene that the spiritual
portrays are set, as the acts and meanings of *Go Down,
Moses* are, in history. After Joseph revealed his identity, he
gave Jacob and his family refuge in Egypt. A generation

later, however, after Jacob and Joseph had died, a new
Pharaoh enslaved the Israelites. They had been long in
bondage when the young Israelite Moses, enraged at how
one of his fellow slaves was being mistreated, struck down
the Egyptian overseer and killed him. News of his act
spread, but Israelites did not treat Moses as a hero. He
was threatened with betrayal and fled to the border of
Egypt, to the pastureland on "the side of the wilderness"
(Exodus 3:2). There God, answering the Israelites' prayers
for deliverance, found him and designated him to deliver
Israel from slavery.

> The LORD said, "I have indeed seen the misery of my people
> in Egypt. I have heard their outcry against their slave-
> masters. I have taken heed of their sufferings, and have come
> down to rescue them from the power of Egypt, and to bring
> them up out of that country into a fine, broad land; it is a land
> flowing with milk and honey, the home of Canaanites, Hit-
> tites, Amorites, Perizzites, Hivites, and Jebusites." (Exodus
> 3:7–8)

After years of hard struggle the Israelites did return to
Canaan and dispossessed the other peoples who lived
there.

This history of the Israelites is linear. They left Canaan,
where they had kept themselves isolated from their neigh-
boring tribes, and lived in Egypt as shepherds. The period
of slavery ensued; and finally they followed Moses toward
Canaan once more, toward a land that God now promised
would be theirs.

The Israelites' history is also cyclic: Canaan to Egypt to
Canaan. $X \rightarrow Y \rightarrow Z$ is also $X \rightarrow Y \rightarrow X$, especially since their
history, like that in *Go Down, Moses,* stretches back to the
Garden of Eden and is moving not just toward the return
to Canaan as homeland but toward Canaan as the land of
milk and honey, the Promised Land.

The spiritual also seems to have its own narrative
chorus. It lets Moses speak four words in a direct quotation at the start of the third stanza. Although he doubtless

went on to say to the Pharaoh, "Let my people go,/If not
I'll smite your first born dead,/Let my people go," those
words are not in quotation marks. That lack of punctuation implies that these words are the Lord's words too as
"Thus spoke the Lord" was not. God is apparently the
speaker in the first and last stanzas, and there seems to be
a third-person narrator who reports and judges in the following lines:

> When Israel was in Egypts land
> . . . . . .
> Oppressed so hard they could not stand,
> . . . . . .
> "Thus spoke the Lord," bold Moses said;
>   Let my people go,
> If not I'll smite your first born dead,
>   Let my people go.

The biblical story, like *Go Down, Moses,* is thick with the
rituals and motifs of possession. Joseph owns the coat,
and his brothers dispossess him of it and sell him into
slavery. As viceroy he advises that the Pharaoh collect
extra grain from good harvests to share with the people in
famine. Before revealing himself, Joseph tests his brothers
by means of possessions—for example, he gives them
grain and returns their money, and he has his own silver
goblet put in Benjamin's pack as if the boy had stolen it
and pretends to have him enslaved for the theft. In the
biblical text the Israelites seek to possess the land. God
Himself superintends their quest, whose pattern He
defines when He tells Moses:

> I made a covenant with them to give them Canaan, the land
> where they settled for a time as foreigners. And now I have
> heard the groaning of the Israelites, enslaved by the Egyp-
> tians, and I have called my covenant to mind. Say therefore to
> the Israelites, "I am the Lord. I will release you from your
> labours in Egypt. . . . I will lead you to the land which I swore
> with uplifted hand to give to Abraham, to Isaac and to Jacob. I
> will give it you for your possession." (Exodus 6: 4–8)

The rituals and motifs of possession along with the patterns of the line and the circle come together in the second unanswered question of "The Bear": Has owning irrevocably supplanted holding? The biblical text shows the Israelites seeking to possess the land. *Go Down, Moses,* on the contrary, anticipates not the possession of a land of milk and honey, not the "new Canaan" in which Fonsiba's husband imagines himself dwelling, but simply a land shared by those who inhabit it. The last two stories in *Go Down, Moses* support the implication of "The Bear" that sharing must eventually supplant ownership. "Delta Autumn" confirms what Part 5 of "The Bear" suggested: that relinquishing the wilderness is futile unless the wilderness can somehow be set aside, preserved within the rituals of ownership. Otherwise, the wilderness will recede as roads spread, as lumber companies seek trees to fell, and as farms and towns grow. "Delta Autumn" also discredits the relinquishment of the tamed land. Passing the farm to the Edmondses does not free Ike of the taint of possession nor ameliorate the condition of the dispossessed. Sharing rather than relinquishing is the McCaslin tradition, and Cass's path rather than Ike's seems faithful to the past and promising for the future. Cass's choice has entailed for his heirs as for Cass himself not only sharing land with blacks but sharing life with them too. Fabula and history show the dispossessed transformed from property to people and then to subordinate members of the McCaslin family. After the Edmondses have acquired the farm, the "black" members of the family rise within the family toward equality and even superiority in status. Lucas's attitudes are the best gauge of this rise:he respects Cass, treats Zack as an equal, and looks down on Roth—who is younger, "woman-made," and an Edmonds—so much that Lucas does "not even bother to remember not to call him mister" (116). The story "Go Down, Moses" extends the rituals of sharing beyond the McCaslin family into the broader society and thereby implies hope for the future. Although the history of possession has divided mankind by juxtaposing the owners, the dispossessed, the enslaved, and the holders against one another, that history apparently leads ineluctably toward the condensation represented by sharing, mixing, and mutual involvement.

If the pattern of history in Go Down, Moses is both linear and cyclic, then one set of the ultimate juxtapositions of the narrative, the line and the circle, has been condensed. If the other set, history and myth, can be joined, that union would be the height of paradoxical condensation for Go Down, Moses. The title's allusion to Moses again provides a way to pursue the book's meaning. In the biblical story the Israelites will, with God's blessing, conquer Canaan and dispossess its inhabitants. In Go Down, Moses, on the contrary, God has rejected possession and oversees a pattern that leads toward relinquishing the wilderness and sharing the tamed land. Thus Go Down, Moses attains, as the Bible of course does too, a mythic vision in which all history is encompassed and unified by God's purpose. Go Down, Moses thus condenses its patterns of action into a single and therefore paradoxical union of the line and the circle, history and myth.

As its actions followed the dynamic forms of juxtaposition and condensation, of the line of history and the circle of myth, so the patterns of meaning in Go Down, Moses take shape in the static forms of juxtaposition X/Y and condensation X = Y. These are the ultimate patterns of meaning for the narrative, and they are also joined paradoxically. From beginning to end the narrative has juxtaposed and condensed such opposites as elder and younger, male and female, master and servant, and black, white, and Indian. The motif of the family has distinguished roles and relationships and has expanded along three lines: the legitimate, white, male line of descent from Carothers McCaslin through Buck and Buddy to Ike; the legitimate, white, female line of Edmondses descended from old Carothers' daughter; and the illegitimate, "black," male line of Beauchamps. With the birth of the boy in "Delta Autumn" those lines come together. Society contracts into family.

On the other hand, in "Go Down, Moses" family expands into society. The book's last story, by reversing the perspective, offers a different view of familial condensation, the extension of the family's branches further and further into the surrounding society—from Lucas through Molly to her brother Hamp, from Hamp to his wife, from Molly to Miss Worsham through the childhood she shared with Molly, and from Hamp to Miss Worsham because he descended from her father's slaves—so that by the end of the narrative the tips of these branches are brushing Stevens, the editor, the census-taker, and the people of Jefferson.

The fundamental pattern of *Go Down, Moses* is thus the paradox. The narrative affirms the static and dynamic patterns of juxtaposition and condensation. It demonstrates that while possession, which destroys what it tries to keep, can preserve the wilderness it relinquishes and the tamed land it shares, the mythic communal holding, lost forever when men first claimed the power of ownership, is nevertheless being restored through relinquishment and sharing. The mythic brotherhood, likewise irrevocably lost, is being replaced through the progressive interpenetration of family and society. Through these processes, according to *Go Down, Moses*, both myth and history are working toward the freeing of mankind; and both God and man are saying with one voice, "Let my people go." These paradoxical patterns are the threads cable-strong that bind *Go Down, Moses* together.

List of Works Cited

Beck, Warren. *Faulkner*. Madison: University of Wisconsin Press, 1976.

Blotner, Joseph. *Faulkner: A Biography*. New York: Random House, 1974.

Brooks, Cleanth. *William Faulkner: The Yoknapatawpha Country*. New Haven, Conn.: Yale University Press, 1963.

Culler, Jonathan. *Structuralist Poetics*. Ithaca, N.Y.: Cornell University Press, 1975.

Early, James. *The Making of Go Down, Moses*. Dallas, Tex.: Southern Methodist University Press, 1972.

Faulkner, William. "The Bear." *The Saturday Evening Post*, May 9, 1942, pp. 30-31 and 74-76.

———. "Go Down, Moses." *Collier's*, January 25, 1941, pp. 19–20 and 45–46.

———. *Go Down, Moses*. New York: Modern Library, 1940.

———. "Gold Is Not Always." *The Atlantic Monthly*, November 1940, pp. 563–70.

———. "Lion." *Harper's Monthly Magazine*, December 1935, pp. 67–77.

———. "The Old People." *Harper's Monthly Magazine*, September 1940, pp. 418–25.

———. "Pantaloon in Black." *Harper's Monthly Magazine*, October 1940, pp. 501–13.

———. "A Point of Law." *Collier's*, June 22, 1940, pp. 19–21 and 30–32.

Frye, Northrop. *Anatomy of Criticism: Four Essays*. Princeton, N.J.: Princeton University Press, 1957.

Gwynn, Frederick L., and Blotner, Joseph L. *Faulkner in the University: Class Conferences at the University of Virginia, 1957–1958*. New York: Vintage Books, 1959.

Hoffman, Frederick J. *William Faulkner.* New Haven, Conn.: Twayne Publishers, 1966.

Jakobson, Roman. "Two Aspects of Language: Metaphor and Metonymy," from *Fundamentals of Language* by Roman Jakobson and Morris Halle. Reprinted in *European Literary Theory and Practice,* edited by Vernon W. Gras. New York: Dell Publishing Co., 1973.

Johnson, James Weldon. *The Book of American Negro Spirituals.* New York: Viking Press, 1923.

Klotz, Marvin. "Procrustean Revision in Faulkner's *Go Down, Moses.*" *American Literature,* March 1965, pp. 1–16.

Millgate, Jane. "Short Story into Novel: Faulkner's Reworking of 'Gold Is Not Always.'" *English Studies,* August 1964, pp. 310–17.

Millgate, Michael. *The Achievement of William Faulkner.* New York: Random House, 1965.

The New English Bible. Samuel Sandmel, general editor. New York: Oxford University Press, 1976.

Reed, Joseph W., Jr. *Faulkner's Narrative.* New Haven, Conn.: Yale University Press, 1973.

Stewart, David H. "The Purpose of Faulkner's Ike." *Criticism* 3 (Fall 1961): 333–42.

Sultan, Stanley. "Call Me Ishmael: The Hagiography of Isaac McCaslin." *Texas Studies in Language and Literature,* Spring 1961, pp. 50–66.

Taylor, Walter F., Jr. "Let My People Go: The White Man's Heritage in *Go Down, Moses.*" *South Atlantic Quarterly,* Winter 1959, pp. 20–32.

Tick, Stanley. "The Unity of *Go Down, Moses.*" *Twentieth Century Literature,* July 1962, pp. 67–73.

Trilling, Lionel. "The McCaslins of Mississippi." *The Nation,* May 30, 1942, pp. 632–33.

Vickery, Olga W. *The Novels of William Faulkner: A Critical Interpretation.* Baton Rouge: Louisiana State University Press, 1964.

Wertenbaker, Thomas J., Jr. "Faulkner's Point of View and the Chronicle of Ike McCaslin." *College English,* December 1962, pp. 169–83.

Index

193